The Joy of Walking

Jack Scagnetti
Foreword by Keith E. Kenyon, M. D.

Published by
Melvin Powers
WILSHIRE BOOK COMPANY
12015 Sherman Road
No. Hollywood, California 91605
Telephone: (213) 875-1711

Printed by

HAL LEIGHTON PRINTING COMPANY
P.O. Box 3952
North Hollywood, California 91605
Telephone: (213) 983-1105

Printed in the United States of America
Library of Congress Catalog Card Number: 79-65633
ISBN 0-87980-370-3

ACKNOWLEDGMENTS

Special thanks to my parents who taught me how to walk when I was nine months old and who allowed me to walk miles with my friends to matinee movies and other places when I was in my pre-teens. I wish to thank the following: American Heart Association, U.S. Department of Health, Education and Welfare, the President's Council on Physical Fitness and Sports, Herb Golinsky of the E.J. Marshall Co. (maker of The Walking Stick), Insurance Information Institute, Health Insurance Institute, The Footwear Council, Blue Cross Association, Linda Lyngheim, Linda Frances Marie, Gail Ganley Steele, Shannon Christie, Lois Greenwald, Lorraine Davey, Pat Hilliger, Hugh and Julie Smith, Michele Lewis, Francette Sarver, Paul and Fay Ganley, Gordon Buchanan, William Anderson, Jill Peterson, Lois Greenwald, Bud Gatlin, Jack Ong, Rita Faul, Pam Faul, Sarah Goodwin, Richard and Dorothy Hundley, Deborah Smith, Jack and Barbro Adler, Robert Rodale, Jack Catran, Elliot Teplitz, Ann Marie Capka, Susan Bekkar, Harmon Frankenberg, Enisse Chimes, Dr. Keith E. Kenyon, Jr., and Craig Scagnetti.

COVER PHOTOGRAPH

Photo by Bud Gatlin, Universal Photographers, North Hollywood, California. Models: Linda Frances Marie and Harmon Frankenberg.

Author Jack Scagnetti, former U.S. Army Infantryman, maintains military style walk in brisk pace through a park.

ABOUT THE AUTHOR

Jack Scagnetti is a health enthusiast who has done a lot of walking throughout his life, including two and a half years in the United States Army's Infantry.

A former newspaper sports reporter and columnist, and managing editor of a weekly newspaper, he worked for several years as a public relations director, promoter and business manager of a private athletic and social club in Detroit. Moving to California in 1958, he became public relations and promotion director for a chain of bowling centers. From 1966-1968 he served as editorial director of a group of national automotive magazines.

Since 1968 he has been a free-lance writer and photographer, authoring more than 1,000 national magazine articles and 12 books (six of the books are on how-to techniques in sports subjects).

CONTENTS

FOREWORD

Walking, which is something most people can do, is one of the finest exercises for relaxation and health. I highly recommend it as a means of attaining physical fitness.

While jogging and running are good forms of exercise for persons in excellent physical condition, it cannot be done by the many millions of people who suffer from arthritic problems, those with back injuries, foot or leg impairments or heart disease. However, most of these people can walk and I, in my medical practice, urge many such patients to do so, including those with coronary heart disease. Walking can actually help arthritic people (that is, if they're not crippled) because it exercises the joints and improves circulation.

Individuals in good physical condition can walk at a brisk pace. It is not only good for exercising and toning muscles but it is a valuable aid to cardiovascular fitness. It strengthens the heart and lungs, helps to lower blood pressure, and decreases cholesterol and triglycerides associated with coronary disease. When walking is done properly and is associated with proper diet, it can help reduce weight, enabling one to make the best use of fats and sugars (carbohydrates).

I would not advise people to walk in Olympic style as not many are capable of doing it. In Olympic walking, you are extending yourself with an extra stride of 10 to 16 inches which enables you to walk a mile only about three minutes slower than running it. An ordinary walker covers a mile in 12 to 15 minutes. A brisk pace is considered one mile in about 11 minutes and that's a stride that can do you much good if you walk long enough and do it on a regular basis. I advise people to walk twice a day—in the morning before going to work and in the evening before bedtime. You can supplement that by walking on your lunch hour or to various errands. I quite often walk to the grocery store. Too many people have sedentary jobs that provide them with very little exercise, and so they should walk every chance they get.

People not in good physical condition can nevertheless walk. They should stop their walk when they get tired and rest awhile. Each individual has to gauge one's own limitations on distance and pace. If you find that you can only stroll, that's fine, too, as it can be a very relaxing exercise. Relaxation is always beneficial to health.

While walking is admittedly less effective on a time basis than jogging or running, you are exercising the same muscles when you walk, especially if you swing your arms (which I recommend for the most benefit). All you have to do is walk perhaps three times as long as you would jog to gain mutual fitness benefits.

Walking sticks and canes are highly recommended because they help you to exercise your arms and shoulders. I advise switching from one arm to the other during various intervals in your walk. Actually, two walking sticks or canes are ideal for walking for exercise that will do you the most good. It may look ridiculous, but as you propel yourself forward, you're exercising not only your arms and shoulders but virtually every muscle in your body. It's like walking on all fours and it's better than bicycling.

One final tip: when you walk, always try to do it as much as possible while away from vehicle exhaust fumes. The walk will be healthier.

—KEITH E. KENYON, JR., M.D.

NOTE: For the past 12 years, Dr. Keith E. Kenyon, Jr. has devoted much of the time he has free from his medical practice to work on inventions that would provide an alternative source of energy. One of his inventions is a lightweight, inexpensive disc armature generator. He believes a potential new source of energy is the ability to extract highly usable electricity from the space immediately around us—solar or radiant energy. Dr. Kenyon says the complete physician must look for ways to improve the environment—so we can all walk in fresh air, not polluted air that so many of us encounter today.

Chapter

1

INTRODUCING THE JOY OF WALKING

Walk while ye have the light, lest darkness come upon you.
—St. John, XII:35

Walking is the most popular form of exercise, drawing 34 million of the 90 million participants in the pursuit of the national pastime of physical fitness in America. Those figures, released in 1979 by Louis Harris and Associates, Inc., a famous polling firm, may surprise some people because they read and hear so much about the many millions who run for exercise. That's because running is the fastest growing physical fitness activity, attracting 17 million.

Many observers of the national fitness scene are predicting that walking is destined to become even more popular in the months and years ahead. There are some obvious reasons for this forecast:

—Running/jogging is not for everybody. Some people find it boring, difficult, tiresome and physically dangerous.

—Tennis and golf, with some 27 million devotees, continually lose participants because of crowded courts and greens. Who wants to sit and wait to play?

—Calisthenics, with 17 million devotees, will quite likely

never get as many followers as walking because calisthenics can become dull and tiresome and require discipline to continue on a regular basis.

—This book is not anti-running or anti any physical fitness activity. If you enjoy running/jogging, tennis, racquetball, golf, swimming, bowling, bicycling, gymnastics, weight lifting, etc. and find the time to do it—and derive some benefits—keep it up. The beauty about walking is that you can enjoy it, too, without giving up your favorite sport. Moreover, walking will play an important role in conditioning you for your other forms of exercise.

—Walking is something you can easily do in your daily life without special scheduling or waiting around or incurring any expenses. The only expense would be a few extra dollars each year in having your shoes repaired and, if you follow this book's advice, optional investment in a walking stick.

—Walking is an exercise that anybody who can walk can do. You can be overweight, suffer from several physical ailments, and be very old and still participate.

—Walking cannot be cancelled by the weather. Properly clothed, you can walk in the rain and snow and hot or cold climate—and enjoy it.

—Walking more often appears destined to become a necessity because of the rising costs and scarcity of gasoline nearing the $1 per gallon mark; one can readily see that money can be saved by walking to some neighborhood errands rather than taking the family car.

If more and more millions of people take up walking as a form of exercise and of saving some much-needed gasoline, the result would be a healthier America and a nation that could reduce its fuel consumption to where gas rationing could be avoided. Sounds like a simple formula to solve two important problems: (1) fitness, which in turn enables people to be more productive in their work and happier in their daily lives, and (2) fuel conservation. Sometimes the most simple of solutions are

Skyrocketing gasoline prices and Sunday closings of many gas stations are emptying streets of traffic and adding more walkers. Prices now near $1 gallon.

"Four legs, two legs, together we walk, a friend with a friend," remarked poet William Anderson when he saw author's photo.

not pursued. And this is one that won't cost the government or the public any money.

There's an added benefit: doing away with all those short stop-and-go errands to the corner shopping center, the post office, barber shop, drug store, etc. can also reduce the amount of air pollution while relieving some traffic congestion—if enough of us do it. Federal Environmental Protection Agency officials say a 30% reduction in the number of such small trips taken, along with a 30% reduction in vehicle miles traveled, would yield a 10% reduction in smog or ozone levels in Southern California. (Many other areas of the country also have smog problems.) Officials say pollution emissions are highest when a car engine starts cold.

There are plenty of benefits in walking—particularly health wise as you will read further on in this book—but let's not overlook one very important one: joy. Yes, you can find much joy in walking. One of the greatest dangers to health is stress. What is stress? Stress is your body's mental, physical and chemical reactions to the many circumstances that bombard your body daily at home, on the job and your environment. Stress is caused by situations which make you feel irritated, frightened, confused, excited, or endangered.

Walking can help relieve moments of stress, make you feel better mentally and that, in turn, aids you physically. A mind free of stress and a body that is healthy will more often than not equal joy. Such a person will definitely enjoy more things in life. That includes sex. Walking is certainly not a cure-all for sex problems, but it can be employed as a means of relaxation, stimulating circulation of the blood and opportunity for couples talking things out. If your mind is relaxed and your body feels good, the combination should spark more interest in sex.

If you read any of the several books written on running and jogging, you are aware of the many claims that have been made for those sports. If you've read them and if you are a runner yourself or an ex-runner, then you also know about the physical problems one can incur in running: runner's knee, foot problems (heel pain, heel spur, ankle problems, shin splints, blisters, stress fractures, bone bruises), muscle soreness, side stitch and cramps. Walkers aren't faced with most of those problems.

But let me repeat again: this is not an anti-running book. Some people just find running is not for them, either because of some of those aforegoing physical problems or their physical condition is such that it becomes difficult. For others, they find no joy in running. I was one of the early joggers and runners, back in 1967-68, but gave it up mostly because I lost too much weight. I also found it difficult to maintain a specific schedule of when to run and, to me, running was boring.

I have always been a walker. In my boyhood days, I lived near a wooded area and many of us took long walks through those woods' trails, enjoying the trees, birds and glimpses of wild animals. We would walk three miles or more to a movie theatre on a Saturday afternoon and walk the same distance back. Some of our parents didn't own automobiles and even if they did, we didn't think it was proper to ask them to drive us when we were perfectly capable and healthy enough to walk. This was in Detroit, where the weather could get quite cold. We walked several blocks to attend grade school and later quite often walked three miles to high school. I can say this: walking to school meant you arrived there wide awake and alert. Not many of today's youth walk to school if it's more than a few blocks.

The walking I did as a youth proved quite helpful in enabling me to cope with the rigors of the long hikes I had to take when I served in the U.S. Army's Infantry. I still do a lot of walking and I credit walking for playing a vital role in the good health and trim body I've possessed through the years.

If more millions of people get involved in walking, not only as a healthful exercise but as a means of getting to a place, we may find businesses and charities cashing in on walkers just as they have on runners/joggers. Businesses and charities have capitalized on the nationwide market of runners/joggers who

Actress Gail Ganley Steele and businessman Harmon Frankenberg find a walk through a quiet North Hollywood park is enjoyable.

are willing to pay a fee to pursue their exercise in an organized, mass participation event. Why not stage walks for charities? Businesses can offer prizes and T-shirts documenting a walker's participation. It's good advertising and promotion exposure for commercial enterprises. And it would save gasoline.

Of all the reasons for walking, what could be more important than the fact that it is very beneficial to your health?—

—Walking strengthens the heart and lungs, increasing the cardio-pulmonary fitness, as it improves blood circulation throughout the body.

—Walking lowers blood pressure, decreases cholesterol and triglycerides associated with coronary disease.

—Walking is a better tranquilizer than drugs. Walking aids relaxation and sleep.

—Walking helps psychological stability, inducing clear and creative thinking.

—Walking can ward off headaches, aching necks and lower-back pain brought on by stress and tension, which exercise alleviates.

—Walking can enhance your appearance.

—Walking, when combined with proper diet, can help to reduce weight; when performed on a regular basis, it may help the body make the best use of fats and sugars (carbohydrates).

Some studies show that men and women who lead sedentary lives run a higher risk of heart attack than those who get regular exercise. Individuals are advised to have a doctor test them to determine the functional capacity of their cardiovascular system, particularly if they are desiring to start a vigorous exercise program, and the doctor will then prescribe the type and amount of exercise. Few people are ever advised not to walk. Often, those with a heart problem may be told to walk at a slow pace to strengthen the heart. Many a heart attack victim has been helped on the road to recovery by a regular program of walking.

Lovers in love with nature: Lorraine Davey and Pat Hilliger stroll a quiet beach near Malibu, California, at sunset.

Introducing The Joy of Walking

Julie and Hugh Smith "know the way to San Jose" is a leisurely after-dinner stroll. They also walk a lot at golf tournaments.

Chapter

2

WALKING FOR HEALTH

Cardiovascular disease has been on a dramatic upswing in recent decades. Nearly half of the deaths of men in Western countries are caused by diseased hearts and blood vessels. An increasing proportion of women's deaths is also attributed to heart disease—it is the No. 1 killer of women age 40 and up.

Medical research reveals evidence of what contributes to the high death rate by cardiovascular disease: sedentary individuals with diets high in saturated fat, cigarette smoking, and untreated high blood pressure which leads to coronary heart attacks and strokes. Persons who are obese increase their risk of heart attack, especially if they have high blood pressure, high levels of cholesterol in the blood, are heavy smokers and do not exercise. It is the lack of exercise that quite frequently contributes significantly to obesity and high cholesterol levels.

Cardiovascular disease, a term that covers both heart and blood vessel disorders, are responsible for more deaths than all other causes of death combined. The American Heart Association estimates that about 27 million Americans have a cardiovascular disease. Among the disorders of the cardiovascular system are: atherosclerosis, coronary artery disease, stroke, high blood pressure, peripheral vascular disease, rheumatic heart disease, and congenital heart disease.

Atherosclerosis—blobs of fatty and other material on the inside of arteries (these fatty blobs stick to the inner wall)—

makes the artery thick and hard and takes away the elastic stretchiness. Because of fatty deposits on the artery wall, the path for the blood is narrowed and it cuts down blood flow. Blobs of fatty material can even close off the artery, and if that happens, it means no blood flows at all. If the closed artery is in the heart, it results in a heart attack. If the closed artery is one taking blood to the brain, a stroke will occur.

Although the basic cause of atherosclerosis is not known, research has revealed factors that increase its progress: cigarette smoking, amount of animal fat and cholesterol in the diet, hypertension, diabetes, age, stress, heredity and the male sex hormones. Cholesterol is a fat-like material found in many places in the body, including the blood. The human body needs cholesterol but too much can be harmful as it tends to stick to artery walls and causes atherosclerosis.

Cholesterol has been very much in the news and in diet books in recent years. Egg yolks have been reported as containing so much cholesterol that many doctors and dietitians have recommended reducing the consumption of them to two to four per week, depending upon the individual. Some people can get away with eating a lot of eggs without harmful effect. My father, age 90, has always eaten many eggs. He took a spinach and scrambled eggs sandwich to his job at the Ford Motor Co. every day for 25 years. At home, he would also eat eggs scrambled with various vegetables. But he has eaten very little meat and did not use butter or milk (however, cheese, which contains fat, is one of his favorite foods). I'm certain the fact that he always has gotten a lot of exercise has enabled him to decrease the cholesterol levels in his body. He has not owned an automobile since 1927, so has always done a lot of walking in addition to the exercise he got on his factory job and working in his garden, which he still does daily at the age of 90.

In the neighborhood in Detroit where I lived for nearly 30 years, there were many elderly people who did not own cars but did a lot of daily walking—to stores, bus stops, visit friends, and to their social club. Most of them lived to their 80s and 90s. While heredity and other beneficial lifestyle factors contributed to their longevity, I'm certain that I'm not prejudiced in stating that walking was a very important exercise aiding their health. Typical of housewives who did not drive but walked several blocks to do their shopping is my mother, who still walks to shop at age 87.

Apparently, these elderly people—most of whom were of Italian descent and had ancestors who lived long, active lives

A walk on a beach conditions you for your swim and calms the nerves—thanks to scenery, ocean waves and sea gulls.

YOUR HEART AND HOW IT WORKS

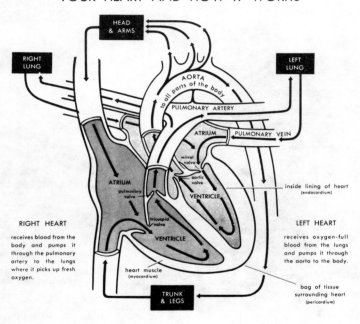

RIGHT HEART

receives blood from the body and pumps it through the pulmonary artery to the lungs where it picks up fresh oxygen.

LEFT HEART

receives oxygen-full blood from the lungs and pumps it through the aorta to the body.

Your heart weighs well under a pound and is only a little larger than your fist, but it is a powerful, long working, hard working organ. Its job is to pump blood to the lungs and to all the body tissues.

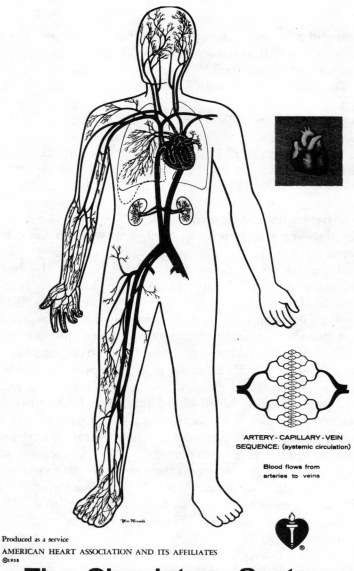

ARTERY - CAPILLARY - VEIN
SEQUENCE: (systemic circulation)

Blood flows from
arteries to veins

Produced as a service
AMERICAN HEART ASSOCIATION AND ITS AFFILIATES
©1958

The Circulatory System

A system of blood vessels carries the blood through the body. These vessels include arteries, veins and capillaries. The heart and all the blood vessels make up the circulatory system.

17

and did a lot of walking—knew that the human body is the only machine that breaks down when *not* in use and functions longer and more efficiently when continually used.

Dr. Paul Dudley White, who was America's most distinguished cardiologist and practiced what he preached all his life until he died in 1973 at the age of 87, said: "My devotion to walking and bicycling has not been an accidental association. Rather, it signifies my deep feeling of the importance of using the leg muscles as an integral part of the maintenance of a proper circulation, as well as a deterrent to cardiovascular disease."

What happens when you walk is that about 30 per cent of the circulation is supported by your leg muscles, and when flexed, these muscles press against the veins in the lower part of the body and force them to pump blood back to the heart. The human body's circulatory system must flow freely to maintain health. If you have smoothly-flowing circulation, it provides protection against dangerous clotting of the blood and the possible development of atherosclerotic plaques in arteries.

Cardiovascular fitness will enable you to exercise vigorously for a long time without tiring and to respond to sudden emotional and physician demands with an economy of heartbeats and only a small rise in blood pressure. With cardiovascular fitness, you have more stamina and can supply more energy to you muscles so they can work harder and longer with less effort than if you were physcially unfit. The physically-fit person naturally puts less strain on the cardiovascular system.

Cardiologists say research revals growing evidence that exercise can decrease a person's chances of suffering a heart attack or having another if he or she has already been stricken, and that if you have a heart attack at all, it will probably be milder if you are basically physically fit.

The muscle tissue of the heart is one of the most muscular structures in a person's body—and, if exercised properly, it can actually imporve its condition. A four-chambered double pump, the heart beats 100,000 times a day while moving 4,300 gallons of oxygen-rich blood through the circulatory system to

Walking up stairs is good for the circulatory system, but persons in poor physical condition will find themselves winded.

19

the entire body. Actually, the body's entire blood supply is about eight pints and is pumped through the vascular system in less than a minute, recirculated continuously throughout the body. The heart beats 60 to 80 times per minute and as it beats, contractions of thick muscle wall pump blood from the heart through 60,000 miles of blood vessels.

There are two pumping stations in the heart: the *right* heart, which receives blood from the body and pumps it through the pulmonary artery to the lungs where it picks up fresh oxygen; the *left* heart, which recieves oxygen-full "recycled" blood from the lungs and pumps it through the aorta to the body. Since the lungs cleanse the blood of waste gas. (carbon dioxide) and provide it with a fresh supply of oxygen, exercise helps to increase—and even enrich—this exchange.

When you exercise, your heart beats much faster. Because the cells of your muscles need extra food and oxygen when you exercise, your heart must beat faster and work harder to bring more blood to your muscles.

Cardiovascular fitness is achieved only by those exercise that significantly increase the blood flow to the working muscles for an extended period of time. Walking is one of the recommended exercises. The longer you walk and the brisker the pace the better it will be for your cardiovascular system. If your lifestyle has been sedentary for many years, you should consult your doctor before you embark on long walks or walks at a fast pace or uphills. Your doctor can give you an exercise tolerance test to determine your exercise program.

Many exercise books feature calisthenics, yet walking is a better exercise for your cardiovascular system. Calisthenics do not make enough demand on the oxygen-consumption process. Neither do weight lifting or isometrics, exercises that contract muscles and build muscle strength but do not strenghen the heart, the lungs or the blood system. The American Heart Association names walking, and hiking, among the activities recommended for cardiovascular fitness (other include jogging/running, bicycling, swimming and active sports or games).

HIGH BLOOD PRESSURE

High blood pressure, also known as hypertension, is associated with increased incidence of heart attack. High blood pressure, which makes the heart work harder, increases the risk of not only having a heart attack but a stroke or kidney failure.

"When high blood pressure is combined with other conditions such as obesity, cigarette smoking, high blood cholesterol levels, or diabetes, the risk of heart attack or stroke is multiplied several times," says the American Heart Association.

Blood pressure is simply the pressure put on the walls of the arteries as the heart pumps blood through them. Your blood pressure varies, going up when you are excited and going down when you rest or are relaxed. When your blood pressure goes up too high and stays there, then you have high blood pressure, or hypertension.

Thus, it should be clear that if exercises—such as walking—help you to relax, smoke less, keep your weight down and generally strengthen your cardiovascular system, then you should exercise.

"Exercise tones the muscles, stimulates the circulation, helps to avoid overweight, and promotes a general sense of well-being," says the American Heart Association. "There is some evidence that the survival rate of heart attack victims is higher in those who have exercised regularly than those who have not."

SMOKING

It is a well publicized fact that autopsy studies reflect that aortic and coronary atherosclerosis are more common and severe in cigarette smokers than in non-smokers. If you're a heavy smoker, the chances are that you are less likely to smoke while you're taking a walk than if you were sitting. Moreover, a heavy smoker usually will get out of breath walking upstairs, uphill or at a brisk pace. This fact has been personally demonstrated to me many times as I have walked with men, heavy smokers, who were huffing and puffing while I, 25 years older than them, breathed nearly at a normal rate. The difference was that my cardiovascular system is in better condition because of never having been a smoker.

Back in 1968 when I first began my career as a free-lance writer, one of my first national magazine articles (published in Rodale Press' *Fitness for Living*) was about doctors and businessmen in their forties and fifties who had taken up jogging to beat the smoking habit. They succeeded in their goals, although all had been very heavy smokers for many years.

One man, a movie cartoonist who saw some of his co-workers die of heart attacks in their 40's and 50's, and who himself was nearly 50 lbs. overweight and heavy smoker, started a jogging program by first walking a mile near the studio where he worked.

Others told how it was incompatible to run and smoke. Knowing that smoking affected their cardiovascular system, they cut down on smoking and finally quit. Another reported how jogging relieved his tension and led him to cut down on his smoking. A golfer, who had been a heavy smoker and complained of feeling very tired and short-winded around the 13th or 14th hole, told how after quitting smoking and getting himself physically fit by jogging, he was able to play 36 holes without tiring.

Can walking help do the same? Yes, if it's done regularly and long enough. It will take longer than jogging/running, but it will be less painful, less expensive and less dangerous.

WEIGHT CONTROL

Can you lose weight by walking and, therefore, fight off the dangers of obesity? Yes. Again, walking done regularly and long enough can burn up calories. The more calories you burn up the more weight you'll lose—if you don't overeat fattening foods.

Normal adult weight is usually reached between the ages of 21 and 25. After that, fewer calories are needed to maintain this normal weight. However, people in their 30's and 40's—and some beyond that age—generally eat as much as they did in their early 20's, and if they become physically less active, they will store the excess calories as fat. If they continue this lifestyle of calorie input with very little calorie output, they will gain more and more weight and eventually become victims of obesity.

All kinds of reducing diets have been introduced the past 25 years, with a plethora of books on the market. However, health experts have issued warnings to avoid extreme reducing diets because they usually leave out foods so essential to health. It makes much more sense to burn up extra calories via exercise than to not eat important foods. You can harm your body by cutting out essential foods.

Some overweight people tend to think of exercise as being something that requires a great deal of time to lose one pound of fat and they shun it. Some obese persons would rather miss a meal than engage in an exercise program. The fact is the fatter one is the more calories he or she will expend doing exercise. The overweight person can require as much as one third more energy during exercise than a person who is of normal weight.

How many times have you heard overweight persons say: "Why exercise? It gives me a bigger appetite."

Naturally, when you expend extra energy, your appetite is increased. However, in most adults the weight will remain relatively constant if exercise is up to the limit of their endurance. A lot depends upon the extent of the exercise. If you over-exercise and become exhausted and eat less, you'll lose weight.

A lean person in good condition may eat more following increased activity, but the exercise will burn up the extra calories consumed. However, the obese person does not react that way to exercise. The obese person's appetite will increase only if the exercise is to excess—because the overly fat have large stores of fat and, therefore, moderate exercise does not stimulate the appetite.

The ideal situation is get your appetite-regulating mechanism attuned so that food intake is matched with energy outgo. If your calorie input is high because you either eat more or favor foods with more calories, you would, of course, have to exercise longer and more regularly to burn up those calories. For example, if you had a donut for breakfast, you would have to walk 29 minutes to burn up the donut's 151 calories; if you ate a boiled egg, which is only 77 calories, you would need to walk only about half as long—15 minutes. This is based on a formula of energy cost of walking for a 150-lb. individual at 5.2 calories per *minute* at 3.5 mph. On that basis, drinking a milk shake (421 calories) would require that you walk 81 minutes to burn up those calories.

How does walking compare with other moderate exercise activities in energy expenditure? Figures published by the President's Council on Physical Fitness and Sports show that a 150-lb. person would burn up 210 calories per hour walking at 2.5 mph, but by increasing the pace to 3¾ mph, the energy use would be 300 calories per hour. Bicycling at 5.5 mph burns up 210 calories per hour; swimming ¼-mph uses up 300 calories per hour, and bowling 270 calories. Golf, which involves a lot of walking, eats up 250 calories.

The President's Council on Physical Fitness reports that "recent studies seem to indicate that lack of physical activity is more often the cause of overweight than is overeating." The government report said the studies have compared the food

Publicist Dorothy Hundley and husband Richard, limousine service owner, have begun early morning walking program to lose weight.

intake and activity patterns of obese persons with those of normal weight. "Several age levels—teen-age, adults, and older persons—have been studied. In each instance, the findings showed that the obese people did not consume any more calories than their normal-weighted age-mates, but that they were very much less active."

Fat, after all, is stored energy. If you want to get rid of it, you have to expend more energy in physical activity than you consume in food calories. Many people simply can't keep with a diet, so they must rely on exercise to lose weight or, at least, avoid gaining extra pounds. While walking provides a comparatively slow rate of weight loss, it should be noted that when you lose weight slowly, it's easier to keep it off. Moreover, as your skin shrinks, it will adapt better to your new shape.

In a study at the University of California a few years ago, it was found that a group of overweight women who were told to eat whatever they wanted, lost an average of 22 lbs. a year, or nearly a half-pound a week, because they walked up to two to three hours a day.

Adding 30 minutes per day of moderate exercise to your schedule can result in a loss of about 25 lbs. in one year if food consumption remains constant, say medical authorities. If you add *one* extra food item daily that contains about 100 calories— such as a slice of bread, carbonated beverage, two strips of bacon, one fried egg or a serving of potato chips—can add up to 10 extra lbs. in a year if the amount of physical activity is not increased accordingly. That simple fact clearly illustrates that the key to effective weight control is keeping energy intake (food) and activity energy (exercise) in balance. If you are too fat, increasing your physical activity can be just as important as decreasing food intake.

Experts on obesity problems say that the weight you lose from walking is all over your body, not just the muscles being exercised. In using a group of muscles, hormonal signs are fed to every fat cell in the body and these cells release fat molecules

Actress/model Linda Frances Marie can enjoy an ice cream or yogurt cone without gaining weight because of walking exercise.

into the bloodstream. There they go to the exercised muscles to be used as energy-giving fuel.

Eating only a few more calories per day than are expended can result in a substantial weight gain in just a few years. For example, a woman eating an average of only 96 calories per day more than she is expending can gain as much as 50 lbs. in five years. A 25-minute daily walk at a brisk pace can prevent the weight gain.

While it is a fact that a person must walk 35 miles to lose one pound of fat, it should be noted that the 35 miles need not be walked at one time. Walking an additional mile each day for 35 days also will lose that one pound. That's providing your food intake and other physical activity remain the same.

Although the average adult man will burn up 2,400 to 4,500 calories per day, depending upon the kind of exercise he gets, the more active person—male or female—may consume as many as 6,000 calories a day and yet not gain weight because their calorie exercise-expenditure activities equal or exceed the 6,000 calories. This fact was proven a few years ago in an experiment in which a group of university students increased their daily food intake—from 3,000 calories to 6,000—without gaining weight. They achieved this by increasing the amount of daily exercise.

Most athletes have the proper distribution of weight to height not because they were blessed with such bodies or watch their diet. Many athletes are big eaters of fattening type foods yet do not gain weight. They burn up calories not only in their athletic roles but in extra physical activity they generally engage in, such as other sports. I know this from my own personal experience from being in the company of many athletes. Back in the 1950's when I worked as a sports writer and later as business manager of an athletic club that sponsored amateur and semi-professional sports teams, I observed many an athlete who was a big eater and yet kept a neat, trim body. Our club's football, basketball and baseball players would consume huge quantities of pizza and beer after a game, but all they were doing was replacing the calories they had expended in competition. I recall talking to some members of the Detroit Red Wing professional hockey team who would drop into the club after a game and drink several beers just to maintain the weight they had lost during a game.

It takes longer, of course, to burn up a few thousand calories by walking than by more vigorous physical activity, but weight loss can be achieved quickly by walking if it is done for several hours at a brisk pace. This was proven to me when I walked for several hours for five days during the 1978 Glen Campbell Los Angeles Open golf tournament at the Riviera Country Club course while keeping up with PGA tour players to take photographs. I lost five pounds and fell below my normal weight. But by purposely eating pies a few times a week, I soon gained the weight back. In 1979, when I walked less miles during the tournament, I didn't lose any weight.

I recall when Jack Nicklaus was overweight. His calorie intake was more than he was burning up walking the fairways. When he cut his calorie consumption and added tennis to his physical activity, he lost weight. When Nicklaus walks down the fairway, it's always at a very brisk pace. He burns up a considerable amount of calories in walking some 7,000 yards in a round of golf.

If you're an overweight walking golfer and find yourself tiring before the end of the round, one of the reasons is due to the fact that you're carrying excess weight and you're expending more energy than the player whose weight is normal. Once you begin to shed pounds, you'll find that walking up hills is far less tiring and you'll enjoy your round of golf much more.

Exercise is a great remedy for a hangover or headache. I seldom get a headache, but a couple years ago I awoke with a terrible headache and felt very tense. The reason was that I had overeaten, drank too many Scotches and spent too much time in a smoke-filled night club while celebrating the birthday of a friend. I awoke feeling bad because my body was filled with toxins.

Walking for Health

Instead of having a cup of coffee or taking an aspirin (or any of the other relief drugs so widely advertised), I went for a walk in a park. I walked at a rapid pace for one hour and my headache quickly disappeared. My walk had enabled me to get rid of the toxins in my body. As we explained earlier, the red cells in the blood carry oxygen to the muscles of the body, and return waste (carbon dioxide) to the lungs to be expelled—my brisk walk had increased this exchange.

I felt wonderful and ate a hearty breakfast. Later in the day I went for a long bicycle ride and ended my evening with a long walk with my son's dog. I turned what could've been a day of pain and suffering into a very pleasant one. Thanks to my walk!

Virginia Iser keeps a trim figure by walking regularly, whether browsing a shopping mall or in Sierra Club trail walks.

Chapter

3

MIND, BODY AND SOUL

A brisk walk in the morning sun,
With the rays splashing warmth upon
A reason to live. A reason to sing,
A reason to face what the day will bring.

—Shannon Christie

Mental illness is one of the nation's most serious public health problems. Government figures estimate that at any one time nearly 15 per cent of the population needs some form of mental health services and that an estimated $17 million is spent annually for mental health care.

Quoting from the Report of the President's Commission on Mental Health, presented to the President by First Lady Rosalynn Carter, honorary chairperson:

"There are an estimated two million Americans who have been or would be diagnosed as schizophrenic. About one per cent of the population suffers from profound depressive disorders. More than one million Americans have organic psychoses of permanently disabling mental conditions of varying causes. As many as 25 per cent of the population are estimated to suffer from mild to moderate depression, anxiety, insomnia, loneliness, and other emotional disorders."

Writer Jack Catran, Ph.D., scientist and experimental psychologist, takes a brisk daily walk to relax after a long writing session.

Elliot Teplitz, founder of Letterology, walks to clear his mind after a day of working with the meaning of letters in persons' names.

What the figures on mental health problems have to do with walking is simply this: a good percentage of those mental ailments could be avoided if people would seek ways to combat them—and *walking* is, for some, one way to do it. We know that stress and tension have much effect on a person's emotional state. We live in a society where we are bombarded continually with events and environmental impact that cause stress and tension. Stress can hit you in various forms: environmental (such as from excessive heat, cold, noise, crowded conditions, etc.), emotional (argument with a friend, relative, your boss or co-worker, and loss of a loved one), and physiological (when messages from the brain trigger an outpouring of adrenaline from the adrenal glands).

Dr. Lenore R. Zohman, a specialist in the field of cardiopulmonary rehabilitation and a leader among cardiologists in exercise therapy for the post-heart attack patient and preventative exercise for the normal individual, in writing about the ways which exercise training may lead to "cardioprotective resistance," says "there is less 'adrenalin-type' chemical secreted by the body in response to emotional stress than in the unfit person."

When a person is under stress, the body's stress mechanism prepares for action. The hypothalamus (a brain region at the base of the skill) is excited by the stress and that produces a substance that stimulates the pituitary gland to discharge the adrenocorticotrophic hormone (ACTH) into the blood, and the ACTH mobilizes the adrenal glands and that causes signals to rush to all parts of the body. As the adrenalin pours into the bloodstream, the adrenalin increases the heart's rate of pounding and the blood pressure rapidly rises. This causes the heart to demand more oxygen, and respiration is increased.

With the heart pounding, blood pressure up and blood sugar supplying emergency fuel for the muscles, the person under stress is now ready to put his or her body into action.

Some kind of action must be taken to eliminate the stress—you cannot just sit in turmoil. Just moving about a room, pacing the floor, will help. Once you have figured out how to handle the stress situation, the brain has mechanisms for flipping an "off switch" to stop the stress reaction. If you fail to respond with some sort of physical action to stress, it will cause tension. If there is a constant suppression to the natural physical reaction to stress, it places an unnatural strain on your body that can lead to serious consequences for physical and mental health.

Doctors say that stress, if handled poorly, can cause diseases such as hypertension (high blood pressure), asthma, ulcers, an overactive thyroid gland, and rheumatoid arthritis. If uncontrolled, stress can also result in the weakening of organs in the body, including the heart.

Doctors say that many stress diseases are "psychosomatic," a term used to indicate the fact that every illness involves psychological and social along with physical problems. Many people will get a "psychosomatic disease" such as high blood pressure, ulcer, asthma, an overactive thyroid gland or rheumatoid arthritis only when they are psychologically stressed. Some get one disease, while others get a different one because each may have a different inherited weakness which tends to run in the family. People will also vary as to how they react to the same situation. For example, the noise level at a rock concert or disco dance may be disturbing to one person and enjoyable to another. Hot weather may make one very irritable, another will take it in stride.

Learning to relax is the key to avoiding harmful stress and tension. No matter how busy you are, you must take time to relax each day. A good way to accomplish that is simply to take a walk, even if only for a few minutes. It can do much for your mental state, which in turn helps your physical condition.

A world renowned Swedish physiologist, Dr. Per-Olaf Astrand, said he believes patients receive strong emotional support from exercise, particularly walking, and are less depressed.

Gordon Buchanan, construction executive, relaxes with a walk in a park in between hours of studying blueprints.

Real estate salesman William Anderson keeps alert mind by covering some of sales territory by foot rather than driving.

A family argument in the home can be packed with stress and tension. Going for a walk can break that tension, cool the temper and give you a chance to think things out much more clearly. Oftentimes, even a short walk will help—a stroll around your backyard, garden or open outdoor areas of your apartment or condominium complex. The worst thing a person can do when involved in an argument is to jump in the car and drive away. It can prove very dangerous as the person will tend not to pay as much attention to driving and may be temperamental enough to go too fast and recklessly.

Pressures on the job can make you tense and stressful. A short walk to another department or, if working conditions allow, a few minutes' walk in the neighborhood, perhaps to run an errand, can alleviate the tenseness. If you have an hour for lunch, you can perhaps find time to take a walk. I know of engineers at Hughes Aircraft's Culver City, Calif., plant who skip lunch and use the hour for taking brisk walks of nearly five miles. It is a welcome change of pace from their work, which is mostly sitting and in deep concentration, and clears their mind for better thinking when they return refreshed. Moreover, these men, who are in their 40s and 50s, are holding their weight down and keeping themselves physically fit by the walk.

Lunch-hour walking can make workers become more productive. Walking relaxes a tense body, makes the mind sharper and more creative and better able to solve problems. Walking is meditative and therapeutic.

Symptoms of depression are common in America, affecting as many as 20 per cent of the population at any one time. Psychotic depression, excessive elation (mania) and manic-depression are the major disorders. Government statistics reveal that the rates of depression are highest in women, and in non-white, separated and divorced people, the poor and the less educated. Manic-depression is more common among the affluent, afflicts men and women equally, and tends to make those afflicted a suicide risk.

While a walk on the beach is a good way to forget the cares of the day, parks and other places can also provide relaxation.

People who suffer from depression are mostly treated by antidepressant drugs and psychological consultation. But doctors also cite the important role of exercise for relief of depression. In his book, *The Joy of Running* (J. B. Lippincott), Thaddeus Kostrubala, M.D., a psychiatrist, tells how running changed the lives of his patients. He says that "the typical depressed individual wakes up too early, tosses and turns, feels fretful and exhausted in the morning." Dr. Kostrubala tells how running has helped his patients overcome insomnia.

Few doctors will dispute that a brisk walk before bedtime will also do much to help a depressed person sleep better. Dr. Kostrubala, a San Diego psychotherapist, urges psychiatrists to walk with group patients, pointing out that walking is relaxing, meditative and therapeutic.

Doctors find that people who exercise release greater levels of the hormone epinephrine, which is the chemical basis for happy feeling, and since exercise increased the body's level of this hormone, it destroys depression.

People who need alcohol and drugs to reach a state of euphoria—a feeling of well-being, relaxation and happiness—will find that they can do it cheaper through physical activities, and walking is one of them.

Life is filled with situations which cause us to suffer emotions of frustration, anger, discouragement and hostility. Our lives' routines are continually being revised by events that inevitably affect most people, including: death of a relative or close friend, divorce, personal injury or illness, marriage, loss of job, change in jobs, change in financial status, trouble with in-laws, change in living conditions, change in residence, national crisis, sex difficulties, change in work hours or conditions, trouble with boss or other employees, and several other happenings. We have to learn to deal with these happenings—otherwise, its affect on our emotional state could result in damage to our physical condition.

Secretary/model Lois Greenwald relaxes with a fast-paced walk around the block with a happy dog.

Learning to find time to relax amid a personal crisis is the clue to being able to cope with the change, which Alvin Toffler popularized under the title *Future Shock*, defining it as "the distress, both physical and psychological, that arises from an overload of the human organism's physical adaptive systems and its decisionmaking processes."

Each of us has our way of coping with discouragement, frustration, anger and hostility—it could be a hobby, sports activity, reading or music. A long walk is an easy, inexpensive and healthful way of finding quick relaxation—whether after a hard day's work or a personal crisis.

One of the reasons walking helps relieve stress and tension is because it provides you with relaxed breathing, which along with relaxed thinking, is a method of healing. The simple, natural breathing you do while walking acts as circuit breakers for tension. Everytime you inhale, the energy of oxygen is carried by the blood to all parts of your body.

Many people have taken up meditation to achieve relaxation. When we think of meditation, we visualize somebody sitting cross-legged on the floor. But that's not the only way to meditate—you can do it lying down or sitting in a chair. You can also do it by *walking*. When you walk, concentrate on how your body feels—what parts are moving.

Medical studies of persons in meditation have revealed deep relaxation and an increase in brain waves known as alpha waves which are seen during sleep, nearing sleep or relaxation. The studies also report that pain, such as a headache, is diminished when alpha waves are experienced.

Back in the early 1960s, a group of doctors at the Oklahoma Medical Research Foundation reported that emotions can elevate cholesterol, the fatty substance that clogs coronary arteries. Persons under stress and tension can fight it off by exercising—and walking is one of the easiest ways of doing it because it requires little preparation and scheduling compared to other forms of exercise.

More than a decade ago, world famous heart specialist Dr. Paul Dudley White offered this advice: "Physical tiredness produced by exercise which one enjoys is the best relief for tension."

Dr. Nelson Hendler, a Baltimore psychiatrist who operates a pain-and-stress clinic for chronic sufferers, believes there is more of a link between physical and psychological maladies than many doctors are willing to recognize. He says headaches and other chronic pain, such as muscle spasms, can often be manifestations of stress.

"This is the most stressful society man has ever lived in," he said.

Psychosomatic studies, those pertaining to the interrelationship between the mind and the body, indicate that "cerebral accidents" are not simply a quirk of fate. Lack of exercise and nervous tension are prime contributors—along with arteriosclerosis, hypertension and diet—to the cause of strokes. The brain is an integral part of the human body. Although only slightly more than one 50th of a person's body mass, it receives about one-sixth of the blood pumped out by the heart and consumes one-fifth of the entire oxygen supply. Statistics show that 25 per cent of the mental hospital admissions have an altered vascular condition of the brain.

It is a medical fact that emotions affect our muscles; our muscles reflect our emotional problems. If you repeatedly tense your muscles, the muscles' length of contracture is less—and if a shortened muscle is forced to stretch and cannot, it may result in a spasm or tearing. Headaches and back pains, doctors say, are quite often the result of tension usually in people who get very little exercise. Headaches, aching necks and lower back pain are common ailments quite frequently caused by tension rather than organic disease. Underexercised, weak, tense muscles can cause pain in shoulder blades, thighs, legs and arms, too.

Today's stressful society finds too many people clenching their teeth, tensing their muscles, and breathing shallowly—all causing a chain reaction that inevitably leads to headaches, backaches and chronic fatigue. Many of these sufferers make the mistake of thinking relief can be found in a tranquilizing pill or alcohol. Both can become addictive. If people would exercise more, the nation's bill for tranquilizers and sedatives—which now runs more than $200 million a year—could be greatly reduced.

In the 1960s it was common practice for doctors to prescribe drugs to calm the lives of their patients, but in the 1970s—with the plethora of diet and exercise books and programs bombarding the public—many physicians have swung over to a new trend in medicine: prescribing sports instead of drugs.

Dr. Paul Dudley White put it this way: "A five-minute walk is better for the health of anyone not already too ill to walk than all the medicine and philosophy in the world."

The Footwear Council sums up beautifully what walking can do for body, mind and soul:

"Think of the pure pleasure that can come from putting one foot before the other in effortless rhythmic walking!

"Walking is such great fun. For no walk is ever ordinary—no neighborhood or lane is ever the same. Every city pavement, every country path, has vistas to offer the walker. From moment to moment, as the sun rises or sets, the light for seeing is different. Shadows change. Forms and buildings change. The weather changes. Step out in a brisk walk and the mind clears. Your worries are left behind. Anxieties disperse. Energy is renewed.

"For to walk is to escape. There are no telephones to jangle your nerves. Conversation can't distract you. Bad news can't reach you—and you can't reach anyone. Not children, nor parents, nor spouse. You can go where you wish, stop, or change direction at will.

"You can walk to think or (better still) walk *not* to think. And when you walk, you can gawk. It is you that is moving (not your car with its fixed environment). You feel the invigorating motion of air on your face. You see. You hear. You scent. You explore. You discover. You enrich your mind. You uplift your soul—with the changing shifting details of life. There the trees and building tops! There the pattern of narrow streets. There a cloud moving! There a blue jay! There a bird swimming in the harbor water!"

Chapter

4

HOW TO WALK

Human beings have been walking for perhaps a million years. Because it's natural as eating or sleeping, we take walking for granted and never give it much thought.

Many people probably little realize that when one walks, it virtually exercises the whole body, not just the legs. Walking along with a good rhythm going and swinging your arms freely, you are exercising many muscles of the body.

Walking is beneficial to the cardiovascular system and for burning up calories because it requires that you use big muscles below the waist which represent 75 or 80 per cent of the body's total muscle mass. Women need not worry about walking resulting in building up unsightly muscles. They will be pleased to know that walking will tone muscles and give them greater endurance.

When you are walking properly, you are alternately contracting and relaxing most of the big muscles of the body, including those in your feet, thighs, calves, diaphragm, abdomen, buttocks, shoulders and upper torso. Your abdomen muscles tighten and your spine straightens and toughens.

Walking, which has been referred to as animated standing, has been called a science or an art by some people. Like dancing or other art forms, walking is a technique that requires practice to be mastered. There are many ways to walk. People have their own styles, and if the habits they have developed are making them walk poorly, they can change it by training and practice. Actors, actresses and models are trained to walk correctly. Other actors who are larger than life, such as John Wayne and Steve McQueen, need not worry about how they walk— especially if it adds some distinctive flare.

One never pays much attention to walking style because it's something unseen by one's self—unless viewed in a home movie or in the reflection of a store window. There are some things we should all be concerned about in our walking: posture, how we use our feet, and the pace.

POSTURE

Good posture is as important in walking as it is in standing. The basic rule is the one we've all seen stressed by the military: *stomach in, chest out, shoulders back, and head up.* That posture not only makes you look better, but you feel better when you walk that way. You will derive more physical benefits with proper posture. When you walk, forward movement of your body is achieved by a complex series of events in musculoskeletal mechanics, and momentum and stability must be maintained. Walking with a good posture allows you to breathe easier and to strengthen more muscles, particularly those of the abdomen and back.

Doctors tell us that poor posture can put an enormous load on our spinal column and contribute to back pain and poor health. Each individual has an inherent structural balance which must be maintained. A specialist in spine and nerves can help you find your correct posture and maintain it.

Underexercised muscles that are weak and flabby can cause a subluxation in the spinal column. The human body is bilaterally symmetrical (equally balanced on both sides), but if one side is weaker than the other, the back muscles may pull at a misalignment of that column.

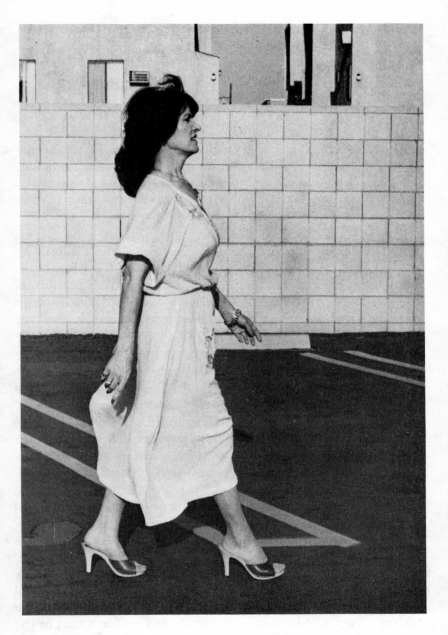

Francette Sarver walks with a correct posture. Women who do so are more attractive and appear taller than they are.

In the poor posture, we usually see the weight carried too far back on the heels, with the pelvis angled backward and thus causing the abdominal area to drop forward and result in a swayback. When the rib section is angled forward too much, it compounds the inward curve of the spine. Rib and pelvic sections must be at the correct angle to assure proper breathing.

When you have your rib section, pelvis and head, along with other body masses, at the correct angle and your body slant is proper, you can feel the weight of your body naturally aligned and balanced in your feet and legs.

Walking is accomplished by a forward inclination of the body while it is supported and driven forward by a backward movement of one leg as the other leg is swung forward to prevent the body from falling. Locomotion is achieved by repetition of these movements. When one leg swings forward, the opposite arm also swings forward and reduces tension in the pelvis and thus stabilizes this region for better balance and rhythm.

The most efficient way to walk, according to studies, is single-line or track walking. During World War II, the British Army made tests to determine the walking capabilities of men women. Using a 70-lb. army pack, the British employed 100 women who weighed approximately 100 lbs. each and 100 men who weighed about 200 lbs. All candidates were in good physical condition and wore straight-last, low-heeled shoes. The experiment revealed that 81 women out of 100 participants were able to carry their packs farther than the 100 men. The reason was the women all walked on a single-line, while the men invariably walked on a double line. Motion picture studies revealed that the single-line walking is more balanced and was accomplished by a slight tilting action in the sacrum—a style in common use by women. Invariably, men were double-track walkers whose center of balance was off balance when a vertical line was drawn from the head to the supporting foot while taking a step. Off-balance walking causes undue strain in the sacral and lumbar region, resulting in men tiring more quickly than women.

Models Ann Capka and Michele Lewis know the importance of good walking posture in their line of work.

49

Lois Greenwald displays medium pace for walking. Swinging arms provides a more healthful exercise.

To walk faster, take a longer stride and swing arms more. Whole foot should be placed on ground, heel first, then toes.

FOOTWORK

Correct footwork is essential to comfortable and healthful walking. The heel of the foot should touch the ground before the ball or toe of the foot. Do not walk on your toes—it will strain muscles in the ankles and calves.

The proper way to walk is with your toes pointing in the same direction as your body. If your toes are pointed outward, so are your hip joints and knees. Outward-pointed toes can hurt your arches. If you walk with toes pointed inward (so-called pigeon-toed), it will place a strain on your knee joints and ankles.

PACE

In order to achieve full *physical* fitness from walking, you must walk faster than you would ordinarily walk. While a walk that is at a strolling pace will help to relax you, it won't give you as much exercise or burn up as many calories as a faster pace.

The average pace is a stride that will cover one mile in about 12 minutes. A brisk pace, on the average, is one mile in about 11 minutes. The U.S. Army calls it a brisk pace when a soldier is walking to a count of 106 strides per minute. If you can increase your pace to 120 per minute, you'll be walking at about four miles per hour. At 130 strides per minute, you will be moving at about four and a half miles per hour, a vigorous pace that is smilar to jogging in exercise benefits. A mile, of course, is 5,280 feet, or about 20 city blocks.

Use the stride that is most comfortable and natural for your leg length and height. Using the basic principal of walking heel-to-toe, simply take a stride that stretches the leg out so that the heel touches down first, and then roll forward on your toes.

Use the stride that is most comfortable and natural for your leg length and height. Brisk pace is one mile in about 11 minutes.

53

How to Walk

To avoid muscle aches, particularly for people who aren't used to doing much walking, it's best to start with short walks and then build up to longer ones.

To quicken your pace, it will require that you tilt your body forwad slightly, thrust harder with your legs and take a longer arm swing. Swinging of your arms adds power to your walk. As the speed of your gait increases, so does the forward lean of your body and the swinging of your arms.

Night strolls before bedtime are good for you and your dog. A city can appear much more beautiful at night.

Chapter

5

WHEN AND WHERE TO WALK

Can two walk together, except they be agreed?
—AMOS III:3

Walking, which is as natural as sleeping or eating, is one of the few exercises and recreational pursuits you can easily work into your life's daily routine without much preparation or use of special equipment.

No matter how busy your schedule, you should be able to work in a couple half-hour walks or three or four 15-minute walks spaced throughout the day. A good way to do it is to simply make walking a part of your life—just as eating, sleeping, working, socializing and plain relaxation. Actually, you can tie in walking with socializing and plan it as part of your relaxation time. Many people can also schedule some walking in with their work. Let's have a look at the possibilities that present themselves quite regularly.

Taking a walk during your lunch hour, either before or after eating, can be quite relaxing and stimulating, especially if you work indoors in a job that involves mostly sitting. A short walk during other breaks in your work schedule, such as the so-called "coffee break," can help you return to work refreshed.

If you live a short distance from work, a mile or two, why not occasionally walk to work? You'll arrive more mentally alert and in better physical condition while saving gasoline and wear and tear on your car. If you live too far to walk, you can park farther from your place of employment and walk the rest of the way. For some people, doing this could save parking fees.

One of the best and easiest ways to get some walking time worked into your life's daily routine is to walk to various errands. Walk to mail a letter, go to the cleaners, drug store, local grocery store for small pickups, bank, library, and various shopping errands. If some of these places are located a little too distant to walk, you can park farther away and go afoot a few blocks. Whenever my work finds me spending several hours sitting and writing, I'll break up the routine by walking to mail a letter. I improve my circulation and arrive back at my typewriter relaxed and with a clearer mind for my writing.

Traditionally, many business people meet and discuss business deals in a restaurant or cocktail lounge. Why not hold a business meeting by walking and talking? Perhaps meet in a park. Then walk onto a restaurant or lounge to celebrate the closing of the business arrangement. A walk-and-talk meeting could be much more relaxing than a session in a smoke-filled room. A smoker is less likely to smoke when he's out walking than if he or she is sitting in a restaurant or cocktail lounge.

Sometimes it appears that the art of talking is becoming extinct. Our lives are monopolized by television, where we sit, look and listen. At cocktail parties, it's mostly small talk. But try walking and talking and you'll find the circulation of the blood in your body will stimulate your mind. And, because you are more relaxed while walking, thoughts come easier. Ideas come your way.

Couples who often quarrel before or after dinner would be wise to take a walk during that time. It's a good way to talk out their differences. A casual stroll through a park can do wonders to cool a hot temper. A walk before dinner makes one more

Walking to neighborhood grocery store, as actress Shannon Christie does here, keeps you in shape and saves gasoline.

relaxed when arriving at the table and can be an aid to digestion. Equally, a walk after dinner can improve digestion. Do not walk strenuously immediately after a big meal; wait a half hour. A slow, casual stroll is recommended rather than a brisk walk. I've found that I feel more comfortable if I take a stroll after a heavy meal, especially those big holiday dinners. You'll feel better and burn up some of those calories you just consumed.

If you increase the forward lean of your body beyond its base of support, it will increase the demands on the calf muscles to counteract the torque of the body weight and you can have sore calf muscles. That's why uphill and downhill walking will tend to make your calves hurt, especially if you're unaccustomed to hill walking.

When going uphill, lean forward slightly and try to maintain the same rhythm as you would on a level surface. In walking downhill, lean forward as this will help to reduce the shock of the steps and keep you from falling.

Don't force your stride as that can result in wasted energy.

Your breathing will naturally and automatically make your lungs inhale and exhale more rapidly when you walk at a rapid pace.

If you plan to walk a mile or more at a brisk pace, it's wise to loosen up a bit with some warmup exercises—unless any work or play activities earlier in the day already took care of that. (Elsewhere in this book are exercises recommended for use with a walking stick, and they can serve the purpose of warmup exercises.) Warmup exercises are more important in cold weather because it takes longer to loosen up muscles.

Unless you are completely out of condition, you should be able to start a walking program by going about a half-hour a day. This can be stepped up to a half-hour twice a day and soon to a full, continuous hour as your muscles strengthen, your feet become tougher and your cardiovascular system improves. On weekends, you can work up to one and half hour to two-hour walks.

Walkers are urged to be extra careful in congested traffic areas, particularly between 3:00 and 6:00 p.m.

Going to the library? Why not go on foot instead of driving? Linda Lyngheim keeps trim figure by walking to various errands.

Mailing a letter at the corner mail box is easier and healthier than getting into your car and polluting the air.

The beauty about a walking program is that you can set up your own, tailor it to your time and needs, go where you want when you wish, and do it all year around. Except for extremely bad weather conditions, you can walk on cold or hot days, windy or wet.

People with pressure-type jobs who arrive home with a tense, uptight feeling can easily relieve that tension by taking a brisk walk before dinner. It's one of the best ways to unwind after a grueling day at the office or shop.

A walk in the evening before going to bed puts you in a more relaxed mood and will help you to sleep better. Doctors recommend exercise for people who suffer from insomnia.

Because exercise stimulates the circulation of the blood, and good circulation is so vital to enjoyment of sex, it is true that a brisk walk before bedtime can improve one's sex life. Also, walking's relaxation effect can affect one's mental outlook and put him or her in a better mood for sex.

Walking with a loved one is an enjoyment too often overlooked today in our mechanized society. The high cost of operating an automobile makes it much more difficult today to enjoy a drive along the countryside with your loved one. Why not take a long walk instead? Not having to concentrate on your driving, you can be freer to talk—memories of the past, plans for the future, hopes and dreams. A walk along a beach, perhaps at sunrise or sunset, is romantic—just as the movies portray it. But so can be a stroll through a park.

Walking with loved ones should also include your children. When my children were in their early, formative years, we always took them for long walks in Yorba Linda, California, where we strolled by orange and lemon groves and enjoyed their fragrant smell. This was a countryside where we would pick up pieces of fallen tree branches and fashion them as a walking stick and where people would ride down the road on horseback and wave with a friendly smile. These walks gave my children healthful exercise and at the same time provided

A walking trip to a newsstand, pausing to browse at the latest magazines, can add purpose and interest to your walk.

Still another regular shopping trip that can be turned into a healthful walk is a trip to the neighborhood drug store.

*Having a destination to reward yourself at the end of your walk makes it more fun.
Enjoy an ice cream, walk away calories.*

them with a chance to enjoy nature and see landscape that is fast disappearing from the American scene as it is replaced by housing tracts.

The walking experience of their early years made it much easier for my children to enjoy walking long distances, such as to high school, when they reached their teens. When my son took up bicycle motocross in his early teens, he already had his legs in a strong condition from walking and this was a plus for him in his bike racing. His strong legs and good wind won him some trophies.

Besides walking with your spouse and children, why not take a walk occasionally with your parents? Elderly people are sometimes neglected because there seems to be little we can enjoy together with them. Many of the retired elderly· spend lonely hours sitting at home watching television and don't get out often enough or receive proper exercise. Going for a walk with them provides you with an opportunity to socialize with them, get them outdoors and benefit from healthful exercise.

One of my favorite ways of walking is with a dog. For several years, I've enjoyed going for walks of two to three miles with my son's dog. The dog thoroughtly enjoys it and looks forward to it. My arrival at my son's home is the dog's signal to run and fetch the lease. Walking is an essential exercise for any dog's health.

A dog is a good companion on a walk—you can take a casual stroll with a dog or choose to walk briskly without hearing a complaint. If you're walking at night, a dog offers you protection from robbery or assault. Women who like to walk in the evening can feel much safer with a dog at their side. I've found that if you walk with a dog, people are more likely to smile or say hello to you than if you were alone or with another person. If your spouse doesn't want to get out and walk, get yourself a dog to go with you.

During the past couple of decades few homes have been constructed with front porches. One of my fondest memories of the neighborhood where I lived in my youth is that every home

You can do a lot of enjoyable walking among nature by threading the fairways to watch your favorites in a golf tournament.

had a front porch and my neighbors could often be found sitting there. As you walked by, you were greeted with a friendly hello or a wave of an arm and hand. The porches contributed much to giving people an opportunity to know their neighbor. Because I always did a lot of walking and had a newspaper route of 680 homes I covered on foot, I got to know my neighbors for several blocks from my home. The American people lost something when rising costs of construction and new architectural designs led to the demise of the front porch. Today, many people don't even know their next-door neighbors—due to no porches and not enough walking.

Speaking of architects, they would be wise to take advice from a panel in 1979 on "Downtown U.S.A.," sponsored by the Southern California chapter of the American Institute of Architects and the Southern Section of the American Institute of Planners. Ms. Ari Sekora, a city planner with the Los Angeles Community Redevelopment Agency, in discussing well-designed buildings: "But on the street level, there is nothing to engage pedestrians, which is too bad. We must improve our streets and plazas so they will attract people." Plazas that were extensions of streets were praised. In New York, developers were urged by the city to deal positively with pedestrians. Recent developments in mid-town Manhattan were created with special street-level effects such as the Citicorp building with its multilevel pedestrian plazas.

The shopping malls that have become popular the past couple of decades are interesting places to get out and walk, if only to window shop and see the latest fashions and goods. Except for the busy Christmas shopping season, I find shopping malls a relaxing place for a casual stroll, especially in the early evening after dinner or at twilight. There's a myriad of stores and they usually include a book store or two where you can browse. What's nice about the malls is that you don't have to breathe gasoline fumes or dodge vehicles.

Walking is always more fun in a mall or a park, but if you have neither conveniently located to you and live in a congested area where the streets are usually filled with auto, truck and motor-cycle traffic, you had better walk cautiously. Dean Childs, assistant director of traffic safety and engineering for the American Automobile Assn. (AAA), recently commented on the national safety scene: "Pedestrian safety has been on the nation's back burner for a long time, even though pedestrians account for almost 20% of the traffic deaths. That's a substantial problem not to get much attention."

Surveys reveal that in some major cities, pedestrian fatalities have accounted for 30 to 50% of the traffic deaths. The U.S. Department of Transportation reported that 8,000 American pedestrians are killed each year.

The message here is that if the government wants us to drive less to save fuel and if we're going to be doing more walking, let's make our streets safer. Better planning for pedestrians' safety is, indeed, important. In some neighborhoods there is a need for improved street lighting and installation of traffic signals. While we could use more enforcement of laws supporting pedestrians' right of way, there is also the requirement that walkers more fully obey traffic signals.

Surveys show the most dangerous hours for pedestrians are from 3:00 p.m. to 6:00 p.m.

If you're street walking, a good way to avoid traffic congestion would be walk at sunrise before going to work. It's a beautiful time of the day and, in many areas, very quiet and peaceful. Twilight in the summertime is also usually very pleasant in most neighborhoods where traffic dies down by 7:30 or 8:00 p.m. Sunrise and twilight, besides affording scenic views of the sun against the sky, can also mean that for a summer walk you are going to be more cool and comfortable and probably be able to walk much farther.

When and Where to Walk

Walkways of shopping malls are most always safe, comfortable and interesting places to enjoy a relaxing walk.

70

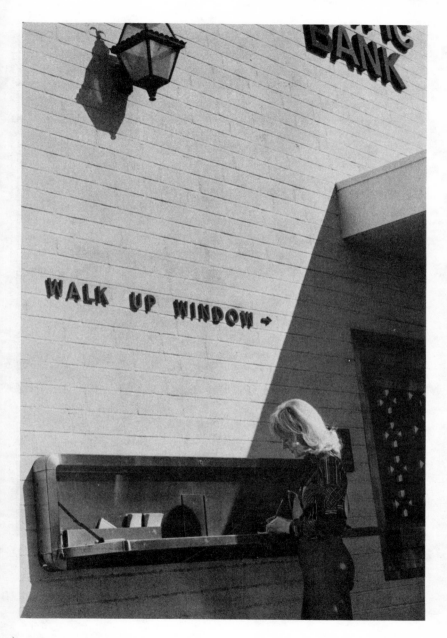

Another weekly errand in which many people can walk to is a trip to your local bank. No parking worries when you walk.

Walking at lunch hour or after dinner to shopping centers gives you exercise and a look at latest fashions.

If you're fortunate enough to live near the beach, it's a wonderful place to walk, especially at sunrise or sunset. The water, the cool breezes and serene atmosphere can do much to put you into a relaxed feeling, not to mention a romantic mood if you're with your loved one. A clean beach, void of broken bottles or other sharp objects, is an ideal place to walk barefoot. Doctors say barefoot walking is excellent exercise for the feet. You can also enjoy a barefoot walk in a park if it's tidy.

I find that if you're walking alone or suggesting a walk with a friend, it's a good idea to set a destination and purpose other than just the chance to walk for exercise or to talk. Some suggestions include walking to a newsstand library or book store, where you can stop and break up the walk while stimulating your mind. Walk to an ice cream store, where you won't feel guilty about the calories because you know you're burning them up, too. Walk along a commercial street and peer into windows of stores or drop in on those that are open and interest you. This is an excellent way to discover new items or "something I've always wanted and couldn't find."

Another desgination-and-purpose idea for a walk is to explore historical areas of your city. Every city abounds with buildings that offer a chance to view a variety of architecture of various decades that have played a historical role in the city's development. Rich architectural heritage exists in downtown areas across the country. You can find the beauty and complexity of the structures quite interesting while at the same time comparing them with nearby modern buildings. It's a chance for discovery and a sense of your town's history.

For those who enjoy walking along natural trails, America has many major historic trails that can make your vacation much more interesting. Viewing historic landscape while walking is a lot cheaper than burning up gasoline when riding in a car. An excellent source of reference to these trails is *The American Walk Book* (E. P. Dutton, $13.95) by Jean George, an expert naturalist and hiker. The book, an illustrated guide to the country's major historical and natural trails, covers the Appalachian Trail, Pacific Crest Trail, Continental Divide Trail, Potomac Heritage Trail, Florida Trail, Grand Canyon Trail, Santa Fe Trail,

When and Where to Walk

Lewis and Clark Trail, Oregon Trail and short trails near cities, and several others.

Not to be overlooked as a way to get in some healthful walking is through golf, either as a player or spectator. If you play golf, try walking instead of riding in a cart. Besides the beneficial exercise, some players say they can concentrate on their game better when they walk. Jack LaLanne, the famous physical fitness expert, golfs frequently and always walks the course. If you're a spectator at a professional golf tournament, you can get in a few miles of walking as you follow your favorite players around the course. It's healthier and more fun—and you see more—if you walk around to the various holes rather than sitting or standing at one location.

Walking up stairs is good for your cardiovascular system. When you only have two or three floors to reach, instead of waiting for an elevator, try walking up the stairway. If you're huffing and puffing when you reach your destination, it's a clue that you're out of condition. Heavy smokers and overweight people will usually find themselves winded after climbing stairs.

WALK WITH ME

Beautiful garden,
Colors sublime,
The rows of roses intertwine.
Seven swans upon a silver lake,
Birds singing in harmony,
green grass, like an emerald sea.
If only you were here,
Like heaven it would be.
But here I am in paradise,
All alone, no other beauty do I see,
Your lovely face always there, to
remind, yes, to remind me.
If to walk with you, through this
enchanted land, no other would I see.
Seven swans upon a silver lake,
near an emerald sea,
God knows this place, do we?

—William Anderson

Chapter

6

FOOT CARE AND WEAR

The human feet are composed of a marvelous complex of bones and muscles that are capable of taking us about 65,000 miles, or more than two and a half times around the earth in our lifetime. Learning how they work and how to care for them will help us to enjoy walking more.

Each foot is comprised of 26 bones—nearly the same number found in the hand. These bones are soft and pliant when we are born and do not finish growing until age 20. Each foot also contains 19 muscles, the tendons of 12 more muscles located in the leg, more than 100 ligaments, and nails that, when trimmed straight across, spare the toes damage. There are, in addition, yards of blood vessels and intricate networks of nerves.

One of the most unique features of the foot is the thick, bone-cushioning sheet of fibrous tissue, called the plantar fascia, which protects the sole from heel to toe. Without it, the foot would quickly become swollen and unusable. The ingenious bone structure of the foot and this protective tissue enables the foot to accept the cumulative impact of nearly 700 tons in a normal day, and continue its job for 70 or more years without caving in.

Women in high heels have an attractive look, but high-heeled shoes can hurt your legs in distance walking.

Shoes made especially for walking, like the Walking Lady, have perfect heel height for walking. Crepe sole adds to comfort.

A good walking shoe is the Hush Puppies brand, a name synonymous with comfortable casual footwear. Principal leather used is brushed, tanned pigskin.

When it's in motion, the foot goes through several basic actions: 1) the heel impact, 2) a transitional horizontal balance phase, and 3) the thrust of the toes, to move us smoothly into a repetition by the opposite foot of the invigorating rhythm that is walking at its healthiest.

A regular brisk walk is rated by podiatrists above running or jogging for maintaining foot fitness, and those same doctors also endorse barefootedness—especially on grass, sand or rugs, but not on hard surfaces. The softer surfaces allow the foot's musculature to flex and strengthen, as it was meant by nature to do.

Civilized man's mania for paving every surface with material unsuitable for tender feet is one of the factors contributing to the 50 odd ailments the human foot is heir to.

Normally, the bones, tendons and ligaments of the foot function together beautifully, each performing its unique role of accommodating the stresses and muscular movements from the rest of the body. But when the natural positioning within the human foot structure is altered by advancing age, improper shoes, lack of muscle-tone exercise, or by the shock of hard surface impact, heredity, accident or disease, then pain producing ailments set in.

Each year, people suffering from a variety of foot problems pay some 35 million visits to the 7500 men and women who practice podiatry in the United States.

Mid-heel shoes are fine for short walks, as long as they fit comfortably. Avoid platform shoes if you plan to walk much.

The following are some of the more common foot complaints:

Callouses and hard corns—These are build ups of dry skin and anyone can trim them painlessly. Simple remedies can also be helpful. But, podiatrists note that older persons, diabetics, those suffering from peripheral vascular disorders, arthritis or others who experience difficulty treating their own corns should seek professional help.

Soft corns—These arise between the toes as a result of local bone pressure. They should be treated professionally since self-doctoring presents a hazard.

Pain in the ball of the foot—This can be caused by many factors; among them: several neuroma, an enlargement of nerve fibers; excessively high arches; hammer toes; or an excessively shortened Achilles tendon. Sufferers should seek professional assistance for proper treatment.

Itch, rash or pimples—These are skin problems that should be handled by a professional with dermatological expertise. Temporary measures, such as the use of a skin conditioning supplement like DermaTime, can be helpful.

Ingrown toenails—Poorly fitting shoes and socks, deformed nails or an improper pedicure can cause this condition. The proper way to cut the toenails is straight across, leaving the flanges up. A professional pedicure is advisable if, for some reason, the nail continues to grow into the toe or the person, because of disability or age, can't cut his toes properly.

Bunions—This condition occurs when the big toe drifts in the direction of the other toes, sometimes overlapping the second toe, and the head of the first metatarsal bone becomes enlarged. Wearing narrow, pointed shoes can cause this painful condition, and so can hereditary factors. Professional help should always be sought in this situation.

Flat feet—While most parents are apt to mistake a normal pad of fat in their child's feet for flatfootedness, this condition does exist in certain youngsters and is generally hereditary.

Walking barefoot in the park, as screenwriter Jack Ong does, not only is relaxing but is beneficial to health of feet.

Those persons with mild cases can get along on well-constructed shoes or with a plastic arch support called a "cookie." Severe cases require professional care and possibly corrective shoes.

Black toenail—This situation can occur if the nails are too long, causing them to jam forward and create a blood blister under the nail. After cutting the nails back, be sure and cover them or spread Vaseline over them before walking to help avoid blistering the freshly exposed skin. Tight shoes may also cause the toes to jam and create blisters on the ends of the toes as well as under the nails. Shoes that are too big can cause blisters, too, because of the slippage. Several things can happen with a blood blister under the toenail. The blister may go away by itself and the nail return to normal. The nail may be forced away from its bed by the blister, leaving it tender. Or, the pressure from the blister may hurt so much that it has to be relieved. A black nail may result from the hemorrhaging of a blood blister. Severe cases always require professional care.

Tingling in the toes—This is a minor problem frequently caused by nerve pressure resulting from tight shoes.

Curling of the toes—This is an ailment that is usually caused by shoes that fit too tight or too loose. Of the two, looseness is the least dangerous, but the extra room may encourage the toes to curl under, causing tightness in the calf. Wearing an extra pair of socks or using a shoe length appliance may help.

Several of these painful conditions may be relieved by the use of the various types of foot supports that are on the market today. Foot supports provide the assistance needed to help return the foot to a healthier, more natural position within the shoe.

Some foot supports are hand formed to fit your particular foot's shape, size and structure. Others may contain a three-point suspension system that gives a continuous, moving support to all areas of the feet regardless of the type of shoes worn. There are also foot supports to aid those people who need a narrow heel, but width at the ball of the foot, allowing them to wear a normal size shoe and a greater assortment of styles.

Foot supports act as springy shock absorbers, and can help relieve aches, tiredness and cramps in the legs, knees, hips and back.

But, the best way to insure foot fitness is to buy the proper shoes. Your feet require shoes that fit from the moment you purchase them. Podiatrists suggest measuring each foot separately while you're standing, not seated. Then buy for the longer foot.

According to The Footwear Council, you should:

1) Avoid high platforms, extremely high heels and flat sneakers. (For supplementary walks to and from work, or during the lunch hour, the appropriate mid-heel shoes you have chosen for business are fine.)

2) Make sure there is at least a quarter-inch of room in the front of the shoe.

3) Watch that the "toe box" is high enough so there is no rubbing.

4) Look for cushioned heels and soles—for bounce on hard surfaces and traction on slippery ones.

5) For support, feel for a rigid shank between the heel and the ball of the shoe or wear a solid wedge.

6) For long, serious walks wear comfortable shoes that tie, whenever possible. They won't fall off when walking heel to toe, and the simple act of tying is a fitness exercise which helps develop flexibility of the lower back and legs.

Also, according to Dr. Rob Roy McGregor, the Medical Advisor to the Council, "When people wear unsupportive flat shoes, they tend to shuffle. The posture assumed is one of a tottering forward lean. The arms are held in an outward, bent elbow, wobbly position—a picture of precarious balance. Conversely, when appropriate shoes are worn, a heel to toe gait is sponsored. The trunk will be held erect and the arms will swing backward and forward in their normal motion."

Other podiatrists remind us that for long wear comfort, it is vital that the ball of the foot fit snugly into the shoe where the medial (back to front) arch meets the sole, and not, as often happens, just forward of that point. They also suggest sticking with a shoe that has soft, pliable but firm, genuine leather throughout, since leather is naturally porous and lets the foot breathe, something synthetics can't do.

The most appropriate walking shoes, the experts tell us, are those with a mid-heel, cushioned heels and soles for both bounce and traction, a rigid supportive shank and a tie for a snug, comfortable fit. Suitable shoes can also be fashionable and there are many shoes out on the market created and constructed for walking, but with an emphasis on style.

Earth shoes, purchased by over a million Americans in the past few years, are an example of a shoe created specifically for walking. This negative heel shoe was designed to "guide you through a gait called 'pure walking'"—identified as a "smooth rolling motion designed to move you along effortlessly, easily and comfortably." But, researchers have found that the Earth shoe doesn't really alter an individual's way of walking or his balance while standing, and, in fact, some wearers have complained about heel pains when wearing Earth shoes and pain around the metatarsal heads. Researchers attribute these pains to the raised arch area inside the shoe. They do speak favorably, however, of the wide toe area and find no medical reason why Earth shoes should not be worn, providing they are comfortable and are properly fitted.

Athletic shoes have recently enjoyed a tremendous surge in popularity and those shoes designed for walking and running are leading the race. According to a 1979 report by a Chicago-based National Sporting Goods Assn., nearly 11 million pairs of running shoes were sold in 1978 compared to only half a million pairs sold in 1973.

The weekend athlete or everyday walker can now choose a shoe specifically designed for his sport. Today there are shoes for soccer, basketball, tennis, jogging, racquetball, and even for hammer throwing, fencing and parachute jumping. But, the athlete should be aware that shoes designed specifically for one sport, say tennis, should not be worn while participating in another activity, like jogging. Jogging, walking and running are all based on forward motion, tennis is based on a lateral one, and the shoes are manufactured accordingly. Interchanging these shoes may encourage the development of tennis toe, resulting in the loss of a toenail due to the rupture and loss of blood supply to the small vessel beneath the nail. Or you may develop runner's knee, chondromalacia, which is caused by the degeneration of the articular cartilage of the knee cap.

Shoes designed for walking, jogging and running usually contain padding, wedges and heel constructions necessary to help absorb shock. Many are made out of lightweight nylon, have a flared sole for stability and a padded ankle, heel and tongue for comfort. Prices for good walking shoes can range from as little as $16 and go on up to $40, and more.

But, regardless of the cost, make sure you choose the shoe that is designed for your needs and the peculiarities of your feet. Take some time to review the selections available—your feet and legs will appreciate it.

SOCKS

If you plan to do any regular program of walking, by all means invest in some pairs of good socks. Wool is preferred because of comfort and durability. Stay away from 100% nylon but a blend of nylon and orlon is fine. One of the better makes I recommend are the Jobst Enduro Athletic Sox, which is created of 56% orlon, 38% nylon and 6% elastic. The high-bulk orlon cushion foot and ball heel construction resists friction and helps buffer the foot against shock. Jobst offers two versions of its athletic socks: an over-the-calf anti-fatigue medical design to help support tissue, muscles and veins with greater pressure at the ankle and less pressure at the calf and a half-calf pair. Both styles feature a bubble toe to minimize pressure and the double-thick knit cushion sole and heel.

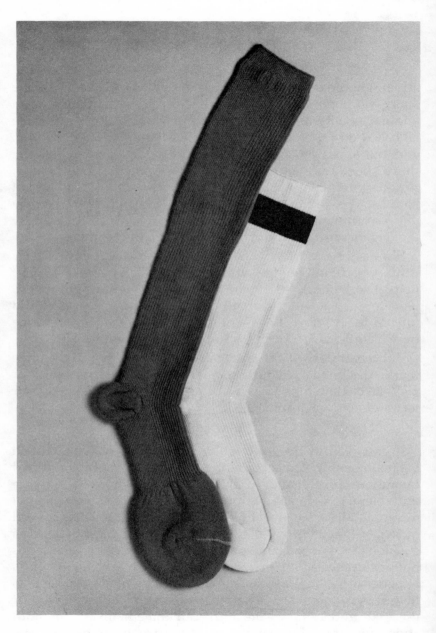

Jobst Enduro Athletic Sox are ideal for distance walking. Bubble toe, ball heel construction, cushion sole aid comfort.

Chapter

7

WALKING WITH THE WEATHER

A walk in the rain,
The smell of fresh air.
Strolling down Fifth and Main,
To see the fashions fair,
An umbrella in hand,
The fun of it all!
Maestro, strike up the band!
"Look at me!" I call,
As I sing, walk and dance in the rain!

—SHANNON CHRISTIE

If you're in fairly good physical condition and dress properly, you can walk in all kinds of weather: hot, cold, windy, rain or snow.

As a youth, I learned to enjoy walking in all kinds of weather in Detroit. Besides walking to school, my newspaper route necessitated that I walk in inclement weather. When you're dressed to fit the weather conditions, it's not difficult and there's a certain challenge to conquering the elements. Later, as an 18-year-old infantryman in the U.S. Army, I was subjected to grueling walks at a brisk pace in hot, humid and dusty climatic conditions. The fact that I had spent a lot of time walking in my grade school and high school years enabled me to cope with the

Cool, comfortable clothing, including a hat for protection from the sun, can make hot weather walking enjoyable.

Sun hats, cool blouses and white slacks are stylish and enable you to be comfortable during warm weather strolls.

long and tedious U.S. Army walks, which involved carrying a heavy pack and an M-1 rifle. We weren't dressed for comfort, but we were physically trained to survive these hikes. There were always, however, inevitable reports of some soldiers dying of heat stroke—just as you read about football players succumbing to it in workouts during the dog days of July and August.

If you're going to do any extensive walking on a hot, humid day, you had (1) be in physical condition to do so and (2) dress properly.

Actually, if the weather is of the intense heat wave type and the humidity is high, a heat stroke can strike a person who is not really exerting the body very much. It commonly strikes aged, chronically ill, alcoholic and obese people and those with heart disease or diabetes. Persons who should be careful include those taking drugs that interfere with thirst recognition or sweat production.

Heat stroke, a true metabolic emergency, is total failure of the body's physiologic heat regulatory mechanisms. It is characterized by a rectal temperature of more than 103 degrees, inability to sweat and impairment of consciousness. The inability of the circulatory system to respond to heat stress results in not enough sweat being produced to cool the body. Doctors say that the heart is the key to a person's ability to cope with heat because it must increase its output in order to pump the hot blood to the skin surface where the heat is then dissipated by sweating.

A person who suffers a heatstroke is in a coma and unresponsive to any external stimulation—sweating usually ceases and their skin is dry, very hot when touched, and flushed. Untreated heatstroke is usually fatal. Less serious heat illness is heat exhaustion, where a person is sweating and may still be conscious but feels weak. Water and rest will help alleviate the problem.

The key to first aid for heatstroke victims is to lower the body temperature as quickly as possible. Get the victim out of the sun, remove his or her clothing, douse the body with water and use clothing or whatever is available to fan the person.

If you're going to do any walking in hot weather, wear light-colored, loose-fitting clothing, and a wide-brimmed hat. Cotton is considerably cooler than synthetics. Definitely avoid plastic or rubberized clothing as such clothing can cause body temperature to rise to a dangerous level because it interferes with evaporation of sweat—the body's major temperature control mechanism during exercise.

Avoid brisk walks between 11:00 a.m. and 2:00 p.m. when the heat is generally at its highest. Take rest breaks in the shade and drink water and other liquids (except alcoholic drinks) freely before and during the walk.

Cold weather should not prevent you from enjoying a walk. Cold climate makes you want to walk briskly to get your blood circulating and warm your body. A vigorous walk when the temperature is low is very stimulating and gives you a feeling of well being. A walk before going to work makes your mind more alert.

Just as runners avoid wearing heavy, bulky garments, so should you if you're doing brisk walking of a half hour or more. Runners prefer several layers of lightweight clothing, but, for walking, only a few layers should suffice. Absorbent, non-irritating underwear is desirable (fishnet wool underwear is recommended for extremely cold weather). Instead of a heavy coat or jacket, it's suggested you wear a turtle neck shirt, preferably wool, and a sweater and windbreaker jacket. If you're going to be walking at such a rapid pace and distance that you'll be working up a sweat, it's best to wear a windbreaker made of cotton poplin, which allows sweat to evaporate without condensing on the inside of the jacket.

If the weather is so cold that you may need another layer, a sweatshirt made of wool or fleece-lined cotton, with a hood, will help keep you warm. Head gear is important in cold weather. Wool is recommended because of the fact it absorbs a great amount of moisture without losing its insulating properties. In very cold weather, a wool or orlon ski mask will come in handy, as well as thermal mittens. Wool socks are ideal for cold

Author's sister, Enisse Chimes, enjoys a walk in the cold and snow of a Detroit, Michigan, winter. She's well prepared.

weather, but they're expensive and difficult to find. They're great for insulation and general comfort. Nylon is not as comfortable, but a blend of nylon/orlon is acceptable in any weather. Look for a pair of socks that offers a cushion sole and heel and a bubble type toe to minimize toe pinch.

A walk in the rain need not be sad if you're prepared for it. Nurse Rita Faul turns back home—she forgot her head scarf.

Walking With the Weather

Walking in the rain is no problem as long as you're properly outfitted in rain gear, including water-resistant shoes. If you're using an umbrella, the plastic see-through type is preferred, especially if you're crossing streets.

Most people avoid walking when the weather is hot or cold, wet or windy, but if you're concerned about keeping up with a regular walking program, don't let the weather stop you. All you have to do is prepare for it and once you've conditioned yourself to walk in all kinds of weather, you'll find it's not that much of a burden. At times, it could even be fun.

Count Yogi, billed as "the world's greatest golfer," still walks tall on the fairway at age 74 rather than ride a cart.

Chapter

8

WALK TODAY FOR A BETTER TOMORROW

*"The only insurance against tomorrow
is what you do today."*

—SIR WILLIAM OSLER

Some 45 per cent of all adult Americans (roughly 49 million of the 109 million total) do not engage in physical fitness activity for the purpose of exercise, says a report from the President's Council on Physical Fitness. According to figures furnished to the President's Council of the National Adult Physical Fitness Survey conducted late in 1972 by Opinion Research Corporation of Princeton, N.J., of the 60 million American men and women who engage in various forms of exercise, nearly 44 million walk for exercise, as compared to more than 18 million who ride bicycles for exercise (as opposed to recreation).

People who do not exercise regularly blame lack of equipment and overcrowded or non-existent facilities. Walking as an exercise program is something everybody can do—from childhood well into their 80's and 90's. There is no economic barrier, no social standard to meet. No schedules to meet and no waiting to use the facilities. The sidewalks, streets, roads, paths and

Sarah Goodwin (left) and Pamela Faul walk home from school. Too many school children ride to school when they could walk.

Walk Today for a Better Tomorrow

Travel writer Jack Adler and wife Barbro take children for a stroll in their neighborhood. Good way to see neighbors.

parks are available whenever you are. There are no fees to pay. And you can usually select a walking site without having to burn precious gasoline to get there.

The fact that walking is so simple, doesn't cost anything (except wear on shoes), there is no game or contest, and no glamor or image to project, probably contributes to the fact that too many people overlook it as a means of keeping physically fit.

One of the tragedies of the past couple of decades is the fact that too many of our nation's children are in poor physical condition. From 1965 to 1975, the physical fitness of boys and girls aged 10 to 17 showed no improvement, according to a report of the U.S. Department of Health, Education and Welfare (HEW).

Schools have not done much to improve the quality of physical education. Some school boards, faced with budget cuts, have drastically reduced physical-education programs. Other schools focus attention on natural athletes, instead of all students.

Too many children are not exercising their bodies; they spend time snacking and watching television, and as a result, not only are they in weak physical condition but overweight. Surveying a 10-state area, the University of Iowa found that 39 per cent of boys and 33 per cent of girls aged 11 to 18 were overweight.

Today many children won't even walk to school. They insist that their parents drive them; others ride a bus, even though it may be less than three-quarters of a mile. Children who walk to school are certainly going to arrive there more mentally alert and in better physical condition than those who ride. Teenagers, particularly, should make an effort to walk to school.

I recall that walking was very much a part of my days as a youth growing up in Detroit. In addition to walking to and from school and to movie theatres a few miles away, my friends and I often explored other areas by foot. Many a mile was hiked through several acres of a wooded area near a salt mine not far from our homes. Walks of three or four miles were done on

Teenagers can get into better physical condition by walking home from school, as Michelle Christie does.

Walk Today for a Better Tomorrow

Accustomed to much walking in pre-teen years, Craig Scagnetti carries over habit in teen years with night walking.

Walking the family dog, Michelle Christie says, is good exercise for the dog and herself.

Sundays to learn more about suburbs outside of Detroit. Another Sunday favorite was a long walk over the Ambassador Bridge that spans the Detroit River and linked it to Windsor, Ontario, in Canada. Walks over bridges can offer you some interesting views of a city. At the age of 13, I often walked a six-mile round trip to deliver my weekly sports column to a community newspaper.

How many teenagers do you know who do much walking? Times have changed.

Not long ago the American Academy of Pediatrics, citing the fact that cardiovascular diseases are developed in childhood, issued an appeal to the nation's school officials to emphasize physical fitness.

Most exercises, including walking, can help fight ailments caused by a lack of exercise (hyokinetic diseases), such as hypertension, anxiety, depression and coronary diseases.

Too many people, young and old, rely on diets to avoid gaining weight. When an extreme diet is carried on too long and not under proper medical supervision, a person can suffer from nutritional problems. "Recent studies indicate that weight reduction through near starvation may be at the expense of valuable body tissues rather than reduction of fat," says the President's Council on Physical Fitness.

"The man or woman who takes regular exercise will maintain a better state of physical fitness, will keep active longer, and is more apt to be resistant to the degenerative diseases of middle and later life, especially diseases of the heart and of the blood vessels," says the President's Council on Physical Fitness.

Most people today do not get enough exercise through their work or life's daily routines. Modern technology has made life easier and far less demanding physically. Electrical and power-operated machines enable us to accomplish things that require little, if any, physical exertion. Thirty or more years ago men and women were much more physically active in their occupations and in physical chores around the home, such as gardening or mowing the lawn. Today many homeowners pay

Beauty queen and television model Jill Peterson walks to keep her figure trim and to relax after photography sessions.

Walking to the tennis courts enables you to arrive loosened up and ready for some fast action, says Lois Greenwald.

someone to maintain landscaping. More men and women are obese today than at the turn of the century, even though caloric intake has decreased since 1900.

If you are one of the millions of Americans who are participating in recreational activities that have become much in vogue the past few years—tennis, racquetball, volleyball, bowling, golf, running, water and snow skiing, and roller skating—the exercise you derive from them may not be quite enough to keep you physically fit. Walking not only can supplement these sports but can serve as a good conditioner for them. All of those sports involve considerable use of the legs and arms, and walking briskly exercises both. Walking can help you develop more quickness of the feet and strengthen leg muscles while also improving your "wind."

People who tire easily and complain of sore legs after a night of disco dancing may be wise to do more walking to condition their legs for better endurance.

LONGEVITY

In recent years, more and more studies have been made by gerontologists into health and aging processes and what affects longevity. While several factors enter into longevity—such as diet, heritage, alcohol, smoking and social background—exercise is always cited as one of the most vital in staying young in mind and body. Approximately one in every 35,000 Americans live to the age of 100.

In areas of the world known for longevity—Hunza in Pakistani-controlled Kashmir, Vilacabama in Ecuador, and the Soviet Caucasus—people work hard and do much vigorous daily walking (essential to their survival in these mountainous agricultural regions). Noted, too, is that these people eat a low-fat, low-protein, natural diet free of additives and preservatives. And they experience a minimum of emotional stress.

When the oldest person in the Soviet Union died in 1979 at the age of 143, it was reported that he was a non-drinker who quit smoking his pipe a year and a half ago. The man, Medzhid

Famous physical fitness expert Jack LaLanne walks entire round of golf rather than riding in a golf car.

Agayev, used to *walk six miles* every day to guard sheep fields of a farm for 120 years until he was 140.

Of all the things that we can control in our lives, say some gerontologists, preventing obesity is the single most important in order to achieve longevity. Overweight people may shorten their lives by 25 years.

Everyone knows somebody who is many years younger than his or her chronological age, not only in the way they look but feel and in their capabilities to perform physical activities of a much younger person. Most everybody knows somebody who looks and is physically less capable than his or her chronological age. In recent years, some doctors have been revealing to their patients the difference between their chronological age and their "risk" age. Doctors use what is known as a health-hazard appraisal, which includes filling out a form about life-style (including smoking, drinking and exercise habits). Information is fed into a computer and it will reveal whether, for example, a person of age 55 may have a "risk" factor (chance of dying) as a person of 65.

The health-hazard appraisal is based on statistics collected over the past 20 years by Dr. Lewis C. Robbins of Health Hazard Appraisal, Inc., and Dr. Jack H. Hall of Methodist Hospital, both in Indianapolis. The doctors are able to compute a person's life expectancy based not on age alone but health risks present in his or her lifestyle. A person can gain back a few years by controlling things—such as smoking, obesity, blood pressure, stress, cholesterol—that are causing their excess health risk. A regular program of walking, therefore, can be of prime importance because as we pointed out earlier in this book, exercise can help avoid many of the diseases that afflict those who are overweight and exercise and relax too little. People can do much themselves to increase their lifespans. Unfortunately, far too many take better care of their cars than their bodies.

Dr. Paul Dudley White summed up the importance of exercise in longevity:

"Physical fitness is vital for the optimal function of the brain, for retardation of the onset of serious atherosclerosis which is beginning to appear in early adult life, and for longevity, and a useful and healthy life for our older citizens."

Jesse L. Steinfeld, M.D., former Surgeon General, PHS, DHEW, Chevy Chase, Md., said:

"As we grow older, interest in intense effort appears to decrease, but activity helps maintain capacity for intense effort and thus helps modify some of the effects of aging. The more regular even a modest investment of exercise, the better health you can expect as a return."

PEOPLE

Throughout history, many world figures have been known as enthusiastic walkers. Writer Henry David Thoreau, who in 1854 wrote *Walden*, a book in celebration of man living in harmony with nature, did much walking during his lifetime.

Harry S. Truman, who served as President of the United States from 1945–1953, was known for his brisk walks not only during his presidency but after his retirement. While President, Truman arose early every day—often as early as 5:30 a.m.—and went for a brisk walk. He was accompanied by Secret Service agents and members of the news media, some of whom had to run to match his rapid pace. He said: "I believe walking will make me live longer." He lived to the age of 88.

Abraham Lincoln was known to spend much time, almost daily, walking the hilltops of Springfield, Illinois.

Supreme Court Justice William O. Douglas once led a walk of 180 miles from Cumberland, Maryland, to Washington, D.C.

Other famous people of history who found joy and comfort in walking included Shakespeare, Aristotle, Oliver Wendell Holmes, Robert Louis Stevenson, Albert Einstein and Sigmund Freud.

When he was released from the hospital after an operation for stomach cancer, actor John Wayne was seen a few weeks later walking down the street outside his home. He was reported going for walks every morning wearing weights on his ankles and wrists to build up his strength.

Author's father, Quinto Scagnetti, always a walker (he gave up driving in 1927) walks to do grocery shopping at the age of 90.

Although his name is virtually synonymous with the automobile, Henry Ford was known to be a walking enthusiast. He lived to the age of 84.

B. F. Skinner, famous behaviorist and author of *Walden Two*, walks two miles to his Harvard office to answer mail.

For many years, Irving Wallace, the famous author, has started his day with a walk. Science-fiction writer Ray Bradbury does not drive, and so many of his short errands are by foot.

In a newspaper interview on tips of how to live a longer, happier life, Bob Hope, 76, said one of his health habits is taking a long walk before bedtime.

Robert Rodale, editor of the health magazine *Prevention*, tells in his book, *The Prevention System for Better Health*, how walking to work was an important part of his fitness program:

"When I was young I put a very low priority on fitness. Exercise just didn't interest me. Then as I got into my thirties, and especially as I became involved in competitive shooting, my motivation to exercise grew. First I tried doing calisthenics, but found that they got boring after a few months. Then I started running, but got a leg injury from pushing myself too hard too fast and gave that up. Several years went by during which I did not exercise at all.

"Then I got to thinking that the distance between my home and office was a perfect distance for a good walk—2.8 miles— and it was largely over country roads with little traffic. So I figured that walking to work and back each day would be a perfect way to get in shape. But a mental adjustment was needed to make the switch from being a driver to a walker. What would I wear? What would I do if it started raining? How would I carry the journals and papers which I usually bring home to read at night? These questions loomed large in my mind, indicating how dependent I had become on the mechanical contrivances of our technological society.

"After considerable planning—equipped with hiking boots, a bright orange coat to warn cars of my presence, and a canvas shoulder bag for my papers—I set out on that first walk. Forty-five minutes later, perspired and tired, I reached the office, feeling as if I had completed a minor expedition. Late that afternoon I dragged myself home by the same route, figuring that my exercise program for the week was complete.

"At first the walk was boring, but as the months and years passed my mind shifted gears. I enjoyed the peacefulness of that 45-minute interlude each morning and afternoon, and the warm-all-over feeling that comes after long and gentle exercise. The boredom was replaced by meditation, and in fact at those times when I have to drive because of very bad weather or the need to have a car at work, I find myself unhappy about missing my walk. Now, I will often walk every day of the week, and average at least four days out of five. Recently I have started using the bicycle for the trip to work and back, especially in the summer.

"Out of all my fitness activity, though, one important lesson has emerged. That is the fantastic benefit that results from spending large amounts of time in fitness-producing activity. Too many people, in my opinion, think of exercise as something best done in a few minutes (or even seconds) a day. Of course, any exercise is better than none, but I have found that fitness is much *easier* to find when you decide to do gentle things like walking and cycling for as long a time each day as possible. You can motivate yourself to exercise that way more easily, because gentle, rhythmic exercising is both relaxing and fun. It is a form of escape from the cares of the day, while the 5-minute calisthenic routine is another constraint, another rigid requirement of the rat-race kind of life. I find it much easier to find an hour or two to walk back and forth to work than to take a couple of minutes to do push-ups or knee-bends, and I get much more benefit from the longer exercise session."

A pleasant walk down a trail with a horse can be very relaxing and provide both you and your horse healthful exercise.

Mr. and Mrs. Paul Ganley, who enjoy dancing, keep their legs in good condition by daily walks.

Exercises with a walking stick can keep your body limber and your muscles toned—without a lot of expensive equipment.

Chapter

WALK WITH A WALKING STICK

Early in this century when the automobile nearly killed the art of walking, men quit carrying walking sticks. Now that millions of Americans are walking for physical fitness and of necessity due to the fuel crisis, the walking stick is making a dramatic comeback.

Herb Golinsky, 54, of Avon, Conn., whose hobby is collecting walking sticks, decided a few years ago to design his own walking stick and to sell it to anyone who wanted one. Today he is selling many of his creations, which he calls The Walking Stick, and which are made by the E.J. Marshall Corporation, Collinsville, Conn.

The Walking Stick is 35 inches long, has a large, round solid hand-rubbed brass knob and a brass tip.

Golinsky ships his walking sticks with a booklet that describes and illustrates 18 exercises that can be done with the stick.

Another booklet explains the need for a walking stick and delves into its early history, and we print it with the permission of Mr. Golinsky and the E.J. Marshall Corporation:

Why walk with the walking stick? Besides the obvious physical reasons like balance, good body control and overall body strength, there are definite psychological benefits to walking with The Walking Stick: To be able to feel at ease walking down a dark lonely street after a hard day's work is not easy in our present society. A man or woman carrying a solid brass and hardwood walking stick is less likely to become the prey of animals or potential attackers. Also, knowing that you have this Walking Stick with you in the car provides you with an increased sense of security. It can make a long walk down a lonely road after a car breakdown much easier.

In the past, many people used to place the walking stick next to the interior entry of their home. Today, this can serve a dual purpose: one, to be handy when you go for a walk and, two, to have in case of intruders.

We do not advocate using the Walking Stick as a club or weapon, but we do think that people have the right to walk without the constant fear of injury. The positive psychological security generated by simply carrying The Walking Stick makes it clear why the walking stick is so popular. Americans are walking more and enjoying it more because of the secure feeling they get walking with their handcrafted Walking Stick.

Down through history, the walking stick in its various manifestations has remained the mark of strength and authority, and the hallmark of men of distinction. From the caveman's club to the bishop's septre, the walking stick has served in functional, ornamental and cermonial roles.

The cavemen used their clubs, the forerunner to the walking stick, as a weapon. And in Biblical times, the staff was used both as protection and support.

During the Middle Ages, the walking stick became a symbol of authority. Judges bore staffs in the exercise of their offices as did monarchs. Kings often had two, the septre proper carried in the right hand, and a staff surmounted by a hand in the attitude of blessing was held in the left.

The walking stick as a "toy of fashion" does not appear until the 15th Century, holding a particular appeal to monarchs. Henry VIII introduced the walking stick as a cane in England.

One of his magnificent gold-garnished pieces had concealed in it a foot-rule, a knife, perfume and a hoard of gold.

Napoleon, also a great lover of walking sticks, had one with a music box attached and in tribute to their emperor many of his followers carried walking sticks which, when held to the light, cast a shadow profile of "The Little Corporal."

It was not until the reign of Louis VIII of France, however, that the fashionably designed walking stick came into vogue. By the reign of Louis XIV it was the mark of a gentleman. Louis XIV found the walking stick functional as well as fashionable. Since he needed to keep his balance on his high heels, he rarely appeared in public without his stick for support.

Through the course of history, men have always been more beautifully dressed than women, with a stronger eye for fashion. It was only natural that they would soon take to the practical and ornamental walking stick.

During the 18th Century, the walking stick had so established itself that it was "as indispensable to the man of the world as his sword was, and as necessary to the lady of fashion as her fan." The proficiency with which one manipulated his walking stick soon became the trademark of a gentleman. In fact, so popular was the walking stick that rules of deportment were established in a book published in 1787: It states you must never hold the walking stick under the arm, or lean on it while standing, nor write with it in the dirt, and finally, never drag your walking stick.

The walking stick was not always treated with such kindness. History has it that when angered while conversing with a subject, Ivan the Terrible would drive the iron spike of his walking stick through the subject's foot, nailing him to the spot.

The dandy of the 18th Century helped to advance this period as "The Age of the Walking Stick," for it was the age of elegance. By the late 19th Century, the walking stick had reached its mass widespread use. At one point, a French newspaper reproduced 22 designs by means of which a walking stick could be adapted as a camera tripod, a painter's easel, a footstool, a chair, a candlestick, a toilet table, and even as a shot gun.

Even those who traditionally shunned the dictates of fashion were taken with the walking stick. Such notables as Voltaire owned 80 walking sticks and Rousseau, a poor man, had 40.

When the walking stick was finally introduced in America, it took a much simpler form. They were usually quite sturdy with simple mountings of ivory, gold or silver.

The walking stick became associated with the intelligentsia and the artists of the time and soon it became "swagger" for the

It was not until the reign of Louis VIII of France that the fashionably designed walking stick came into vogue.

Handcrafted, The Walking Stick has a handle made of solid brass, hand-polished and engineered to withstand 3,000 lbs. of pull. The handle is designed to give proper feel and balance while walking. Each stick is shipped with booklets on care of the stick, history, and illustrated exercises.

With walking stick in hand and a dog at your side, a night walker has a secure feeling.

Englishwomen in the country to carry walking sticks. By the early 20th Century, men walked proudly displaying his stick wherever he went.

Although simpler at first, the American walking sticks soon rivaled their exotic European counterparts. J. P. Morgan, the famous financier, had a walking stick with a built-in battery-powered flashlight. Another marvel of American ingenuity was a walking stick that featured a coin dispenser, a useful accessory in the days of the five-cent cigar. One souvenir walking stick of 1939 contained a rolled-up map of that year's World Fair. Walking sticks were being mass produced by this time and quite a few were manufactured as souvenirs for political conventions, often with a likeness of the leading candidate.

Walking sticks can be fashionable with casual wear, too, in this generation of health-minded walkers.

121

Walk With a Walking Stick

A man or woman carrying a solid brass and hardwood walking stick is less likely to become the prey of animals or attackers.

Today, orthopedic surgeons are urging the use of walking sticks as a valuable aid to prevent fatigue.

With renewed interest in physical fitness and the resurgence of walkers and hikers, the walking stick is again attracting attention.

Men of fashion and practicability have long since recognized the value of this salubrious aid.

The Walking Stick has been carefully designed to meet the needs of our time when walking must become an intrical part of our lives. It is time we rediscovered the importance of the walking stick. Start walking towards good health and a secure feeling with your own Walking Stick.

* * *

The Wilshire Book Company and the author of this book have checked out several walking sticks and find that The Walking Stick by Herb Golinsky of E. J. Marshall Corporation is of superior quality and we highly recommend it.

The Walking Stick is made in the American tradition of meticulous craftsmanship in Collinsville, a quaint New England town in Central Connecticut.

The handle of The Walking Stick is made of solid brass. It is hand-polished and engineered to withstand 3,000 lbs. of pull. The handle is designed to give proper feel and balance while walking. You'll find a special mark at the base of the handle which identifies it as the genuine Walking Stick. This mark insures the increased value of your Walking Stick in time.

The shaft is made of top quality hardwood. It was chosen for its durability and high resistance to impact (This same wood is used for making professional hockey sticks, baseball bats, and fine axe handles). The wood has been treated to withstand the elements and years of constant use. The special finish used to preserve this fine wood will improve with age, giving your Walking Stick a distinguished appearance.

The finial is hand-polished, non-corrosive brass. A replaceable nylon tip insert finishes off The Walking Stick. This tip prevents damage to the wooden shaft or to any surface it comes in contact with.

Walk With a Walking Stick

For the convenience of those who are unable to locate a good walking stick in their neighborhood, the Wilshire Book Company is making The Walking Stick available to readers for $30, which includes all shipping costs and an information booklet and an illustrated exercise booklet. Send your order to: Wilshire Book Company, 12015 Sherman Road, No. Hollywood, California 91605.

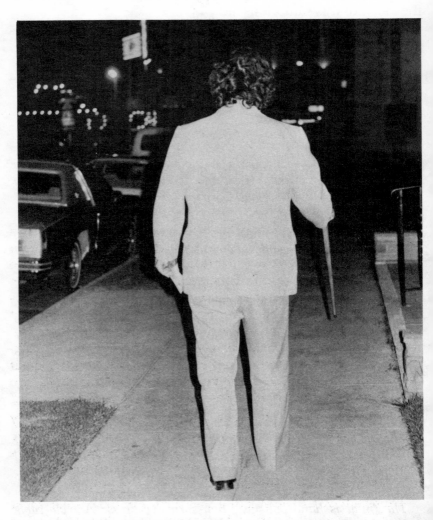

There are psychological benefits to walking with a walking stick, especially at night on a lonely street.

Chapter

10

EXERCISES ON A STICK

The exercises shown here have been designed so that in just a few minutes a day, you can keep your body limber and your muscles toned—without a lot of expensive equipment. They're easy and even fun to do. If you're a normally healthy person between the ages of 15 and 65, you can do these movements without strain or over-exertion. And you can do them just about anywhere. While out walking, at home or in the office. Most important after just one session with The Walking Stick, you'll notice the difference in the way you feel. And this great feeling of fitness is one of the best encouragements there is to continue exercising regularly and to form the "exercise habit."

The exercises described here are not meant to replace any present activities you may have like golf or tennis. Rather they are designed for use between such activities to keep muscles responsive and limber. Then if you do exercise more strenuously, you stand less of a chance of strain or fatigue.

Exercising with The Walking Stick is one of the easiest, most natural ways to start getting in shape and to help you stay that way.

EXERCISES YOU CAN DO WHILE YOU'RE WALKING

1. FOR YOUR NECK, ARMS AND SHOULDERS.

Hold The Walking Stick outstretched in your right hand, eight inches below the brass knob with your arm straight. Slowly swing The Walking Stick as far to your right as possible. As you swing The Walking Stick, turn your neck too, so you're always sighting the head of The Walking Stick. Hold this stretched position to the count of ten. Return your arm and head to center. Repeat four times for each side, work up to eight.

A FEW TIPS TO HELP YOU GET THE MOST OUT OF EXERCISING

1. When possible start with a lateral exercise, such as numbers 1, 3, 5, 9, or 10. Your side muscles are under almost constant tension and should always be warmed up before you begin exercising your upper body. ➤

2. FOR YOUR ARMS AND SHOULDERS.

Hold the bottom of The Walking Stick outstretched in your right hand parallel to ground with arm straight. Rotate The Walking Stick counterclockwise six times in large circles, then clockwise six times in very tight circles. Repeat the series four times for each side, work up to eight.

---

2. **Any time** you do an exercise for one side of your body, always repeat the exercise the same number of times for the other side.

3. Don't rush through these exercises—or any exercise. Give your muscles and joints a chance to work themselves loose and warm up. That way there's much less chance of strain.

4. Do these exercises as regularly as possible. You'll feel better for it. And you'll stay in better shape.

3. FOR YOUR CHEST, ARMS, BACK AND SHOULDERS.

Hold both arms outstretched to your sides with The Walking Stick, held just below brass knob in your right hand. Slowly bring your right hand around until it touches your left. Repeat six times on each side, work up to twelve.

4. FOR YOUR SHOULDERS AND ARMS.

With your arms extended straight forward, hold The Walking Stick vertically with one hand at each end. Rotate 180 degrees clockwise and back five times, then reverse your hands and do same number of times counterclockwise. Repeat series twice, work up to five times.

4A. Perform exercise 4 with both hands in the middle of The Walking Stick.

5. FOR YOUR BACK AND WAIST.

With your shoulders back and your arms bent, place The Walking Stick between your elbows and back. Slowly rotate your upper body first one way, then the other. Do five complete cycles. Repeat twice, work up to fifteen times.

6. FOR YOUR ARMS AND SHOULDERS.

Hold the bottom of The Walking Stick in your right hand, and slowly raise the stick from the ground until your arm and The Walking Stick are horizontal. Hold for a count of ten, let drop. Repeat fifteen times for each side, work up to thirty.

7. FOR YOUR CHEST, ARMS AND SHOULDERS.

With one end of The Walking Stick in each palm, extend your arms directly in front of your body and exert inward (isometric) pressure on The Walking Stick. Lower The Walking Stick until it touches your thighs, then raise it slowly over your head, keeping your arms stiff and always exerting pressure. Slowly lower The Walking Stick to your thighs again. Repeat five times, work up to fifteen.

Exercises on a Stick

8. FOR YOUR ARMS AND SHOULDERS.

Holding The Walking Stick near each end, extend your arms forward. Slowly raise The Walking Stick directly overhead, then bring it down behind your head to rest on your shoulders. Slowly return to original position. Repeat ten times, work up to twenty.

9. FOR YOUR WRISTS.

Hold The Walking Stick about 8" below its head. Bend your arm and twist your wrist so the head of The Walking Stick weaves a figure 8 underneath your arm. Exaggerate this motion as much as possible. Repeat twenty-five times, work up to fifty.

10. FOR YOUR WAIST.

Hold The Walking Stick outstretched in your right hand, in a horizontal position, arm straight. Swing it slowly in the widest possible arc directly over your head and as far to your left side as possible. Swing back slowly. Repeat four times, work up to eight.

11. FOR YOUR CHEST, WRISTS AND GRIP.

Holding The Walking Stick 8″ below brass head, toss it back and forth from hand to hand. Squeeze each time you catch it. Do twenty-five times, work up to fifty.

EXERCISES YOU CAN DO IN YOUR HOME OR OFFICE

12. FOR YOUR STOMACH, BACK AND SHOULDERS.

Lying on your stomach, hold The Walking Stick with your arms outstretched over your head. Slowly raise both arms and head, then lower slowly. Repeat eight times, work up to fifteen.

13. FOR YOUR BACK.

Lie on your back with your knees slightly bent. Place The Walking Stick behind your knees and pull them slowly to your chest. Hold tight, rock back and forth three times, and return to the original position. Repeat three times, work up to five.

14. FOR YOUR WAIST AND BACK.

Standing with your legs slightly apart, hold each end of The Walking Stick behind your back. Bend forward from your hips and bounce your upper body up and down five times. Work up to fifteen.

138

15. FOR YOUR WAIST, BACK AND SHOULDERS.

Standing with your legs slightly apart and your arms extended straight out to your sides, hold The Walking Stick in your right hand. Slowly rotate your upper body first one way as far as you can, then the other. Do five complete cycles. Switch hands and repeat twice for each side, work up to five times.

139

16. FOR YOUR BACK, LEGS AND THIGHS.

Standing with your legs slightly apart, hold The Walking Stick behind your hips. Slide The Walking Stick down to your ankles, and back five times, keeping your legs straight. Repeat three times, work up to five.

17. FOR YOUR UPPER BACK.

Bending from the waist, hold The Walking Stick near the floor. Without straightening your back, bring The Walking Stick to your chest slowly as you force your elbows back. Slowly lower The Walking Stick to the floor. Repeat ten times, work up to fifteen.

18. FOR YOUR WAIST, THIGHS AND LEGS.

With The Walking Stick on the floor, bend from the waist, as you would touching your toes. Pick up The Walking Stick, then straighten your body slowly. Lower the stick slowly to the floor. Repeat ten times, work up to fifteen.

—Reprinted by permission from
the booklet, *Exercising With
The Walking Stick*, by The E. J.
Marshall Corporation,

Chapter

11

MESSAGES FOR WALKERS

A smorgasbord of information on walking:
● *SUGGESTED T-SHIRT MESSAGES FOR WALKERS!*
  —SAVE ENERGY: WALK!
  —WALKING SAVES FUEL
  —LET'S WALK AND TALK
  —WALKING IS FREE
  —WALKERS DON'T POLLUTE
  —WALK TALL
  —WALKING IS LIVING
  —JOY OF WALKING
  —WALK MILES TO LOSE INCHES
  —WALKING IS GOOD FOR THE SOUL
  —WALKING IS CHEAPER
  —WALKERS LIVE LONGER
  —WALK WITH ME
  —WALK TO WORK
  —WALKERS NEVER RUN OUT OF GAS

- *SONG TITLES FEATURING WALKING:*
  - —You'll Never Walk Alone
  - —I Walk Alone
  - —Walking Down Broadway
  - —Walk, Don't Run
  - —Just Walking in the Rain
  - —Walk Hand in Hand
  - —Walk Right In
  - —Walkin' in the Rain
  - —Walk in de Middle of de Road
  - —Walkin' to Missouri
  - —Walk Like a Man
  - —Walk on the Wild Side
  - —Walkin' My Baby Back Home
- *WALKING SUPERSTITIONS:*

Never allow anyone to pass between you and your companion while walking together, as this brings bad luck. If it happens, retrace your steps to the point of separation if you wish to counteract the spell—or; say the words "bread and butter." Never pass an object (such as a pole) if it separates you and your companion; both walk together around it.

Walking under a ladder brings bad luck.

- *WALKING AND SMOKING:*

Famous old advertising slogan: "I'd walk a mile for a Camel."—Camel Cigarettes.

Critical comments today: Anyone who can walk a mile for a cigarette is probably not a heavy smoker. Warning: Walking a mile while smoking a cigarette may be dangerous to your health.

- *CHANGING TIMES:*

New proverb: Why run, when you can walk!

- *OLD PROVERBS:*

Better walk before than behind a police horse.
After dinner sit a while, after supper walk a mile.

They say walk with your head held high. Yes, but look down now and then or you may find yourself in a construction hole.

MOST FEARED NIGHT WALKER: Fredric March starred in the double-title role of Dr. Jekyll and Mr. Hyde (Paramount/MGM release). Note walking stick.

A PERSONAL WORD FROM MELVIN POWERS
PUBLISHER, WILSHIRE BOOK COMPANY

Dear Friend:

My goal is to publish interesting, informative, and inspirational books. You can help me accomplish this **by** answering the following questions, either by phone or **by** mail. Or, if convenient for you, I would welcome the opportunity to visit with you in my office and hear your comments in person.

Did you enjoy reading this book? Why?

Would you enjoy reading another similar book?

What idea in the book impressed you the most?

If applicable to your situation, have you incorporated this idea in your daily life?

Is there a chapter that could serve as a theme for an entire book? Please explain.

If you have an idea for a book, I would welcome discussing it with you. If you already have one in progress, write or call me concerning possible publication. I can be reached at (213) 875-1711 or (213) 983-1105.

Sincerely yours,

MELVIN POWERS

12015 Sherman Road
North Hollywood, California 91605

MELVIN POWERS SELF-IMPROVEMENT LIBRARY

ASTROLOGY

_____ASTROLOGY: HOW TO CHART YOUR HOROSCOPE *Max Heindel* 3.00
_____ASTROLOGY: YOUR PERSONAL SUN-SIGN GUIDE *Beatrice Ryder* 3.00
_____ASTROLOGY FOR EVERYDAY LIVING *Janet Harris* 2.00
_____ASTROLOGY MADE EASY *Astarte* 2.00
_____ASTROLOGY MADE PRACTICAL *Alexandra Kayhle* 3.00
_____ASTROLOGY, ROMANCE, YOU AND THE STARS *Anthony Norvell* 4.00
_____MY WORLD OF ASTROLOGY *Sydney Omarr* 5.00
_____THOUGHT DIAL *Sydney Omarr* 3.00
_____ZODIAC REVEALED *Rupert Gleadow* 2.00

BRIDGE

_____BRIDGE BIDDING MADE EASY *Edwin B. Kantar* 5.00
_____BRIDGE CONVENTIONS *Edwin B. Kantar* 5.00
_____BRIDGE HUMOR *Edwin B. Kantar* 3.00
_____COMPETITIVE BIDDING IN MODERN BRIDGE *Edgar Kaplan* 4.00
_____DEFENSIVE BRIDGE PLAY COMPLETE *Edwin B. Kantar* 10.00
_____HOW TO IMPROVE YOUR BRIDGE *Alfred Sheinwold* 2.00
_____INTRODUCTION TO DEFENDER'S PLAY *Edwin B. Kantar* 3.00
_____SHORT CUT TO WINNING BRIDGE *Alfred Sheinwold* 3.00
_____TEST YOUR BRIDGE PLAY *Edwin B. Kantar* 3.00
_____WINNING DECLARER PLAY *Dorothy Hayden Truscott* 4.00

BUSINESS, STUDY & REFERENCE

_____CONVERSATION MADE EASY *Elliot Russell* 2.00
_____EXAM SECRET *Dennis B. Jackson* 2.00
_____FIX-IT BOOK *Arthur Symons* 2.00
_____HOW TO DEVELOP A BETTER SPEAKING VOICE *M. Hellier* 2.00
_____HOW TO MAKE A FORTUNE IN REAL ESTATE *Albert Winnikoff* 3.00
_____INCREASE YOUR LEARNING POWER *Geoffrey A. Dudley* 2.00
_____MAGIC OF NUMBERS *Robert Tocquet* 2.00
_____PRACTICAL GUIDE TO BETTER CONCENTRATION *Melvin Powers* 2.00
_____PRACTICAL GUIDE TO PUBLIC SPEAKING *Maurice Forley* 3.00
_____7 DAYS TO FASTER READING *William S. Schaill* 2.00
_____SONGWRITERS RHYMING DICTIONARY *Jane Shaw Whitfield* 5.00
_____SPELLING MADE EASY *Lester D. Basch & Dr. Milton Finkelstein* 2.00
_____STUDENT'S GUIDE TO BETTER GRADES *J. A. Rickard* 2.00
_____TEST YOURSELF—Find Your Hidden Talent *Jack Shafer* 2.00
_____YOUR WILL & WHAT TO DO ABOUT IT *Attorney Samuel G. Kling* 3.00

CALLIGRAPHY

_____CALLIGRAPHY—The Art of Beautfiul Writing *Katherine Jeffares* 5.00

CHESS & CHECKERS

_____BEGINNER'S GUIDE TO WINNING CHESS *Fred Reinfeld* 3.00
_____BETTER CHESS—How to Play *Fred Reinfeld* 2.00
_____CHECKERS MADE EASY *Tom Wiswell* 2.00
_____CHESS IN TEN EASY LESSONS *Larry Evans* 3.00
_____CHESS MADE EASY *Milton L. Hanauer* 3.00
_____CHESS MASTERY—A New Approach *Fred Reinfeld* 2.00
_____CHESS PROBLEMS FOR BEGINNERS *edited by Fred Reinfeld* 2.00
_____CHESS SECRETS REVEALED *Fred Reinfeld* 2.00
_____CHESS STRATEGY—An Expert's Guide *Fred Reinfeld* 2.00
_____CHESS TACTICS FOR BEGINNERS *edited by Fred Reinfeld* 2.00
_____CHESS THEORY & PRACTICE *Morry & Mitchell* 2.00
_____HOW TO WIN AT CHECKERS *Fred Reinfeld* 2.00
_____1001 BRILLIANT WAYS TO CHECKMATE *Fred Reinfeld* 3.00
_____1001 WINNING CHESS SACRIFICES & COMBINATIONS *Fred Reinfeld* 3.00
_____SOVIET CHESS *Edited by R. G. Wade* 3.00

COOKERY & HERBS

_____CULPEPER'S HERBAL REMEDIES *Dr. Nicholas Culpeper* 2.00
_____FAST GOURMET COOKBOOK *Poppy Cannon* 2.50
_____GINSENG The Myth & The Truth *Joseph P. Hou* 3.00

—HEALING POWER OF HERBS *May Bethel*	3.00
—HEALING POWER OF NATURAL FOODS *May Bethel*	3.00
—HERB HANDBOOK *Dawn MacLeod*	3.00
—HERBS FOR COOKING AND HEALING *Dr. Donald Law*	2.00
—HERBS FOR HEALTH—How to Grow & Use Them *Louise Evans Doole*	3.00
—HOME GARDEN COOKBOOK—Delicious Natural Food Recipes *Ken Kraft*	3.00
—MEDICAL HERBALIST edited by *Dr. J. R. Yemm*	3.00
—NATURAL FOOD COOKBOOK *Dr. Harry C. Bond*	3.00
—NATURE'S MEDICINES *Richard Lucas*	3.00
—VEGETABLE GARDENING FOR BEGINNERS *Hugh Wiberg*	2.00
—VEGETABLES FOR TODAY'S GARDENS *R. Milton Carleton*	2.00
—VEGETARIAN COOKERY *Janet Walker*	3.00
—VEGETARIAN COOKING MADE EASY & DELECTABLE *Veronica Vezza*	2.00
—VEGETARIAN DELIGHTS—A Happy Cookbook for Health *K. R. Mehta*	2.00
—VEGETARIAN GOURMET COOKBOOK *Joyce McKinnel*	3.00

GAMBLING & POKER

—ADVANCED POKER STRATEGY & WINNING PLAY *A. D. Livingston*	3.00
—HOW NOT TO LOSE AT POKER *Jeffrey Lloyd Castle*	3.00
—HOW TO WIN AT DICE GAMES *Skip Frey*	3.00
—HOW TO WIN AT POKER *Terence Reese & Anthony T. Watkins*	2.00
—SECRETS OF WINNING POKER *George S. Coffin*	3.00
—WINNING AT CRAPS *Dr. Lloyd T. Commins*	3.00
—WINNING AT GIN *Chester Wander & Cy Rice*	3.00
—WINNING AT POKER—An Expert's Guide *John Archer*	3.00
—WINNING AT 21—An Expert's Guide *John Archer*	3.00
—WINNING POKER SYSTEMS *Norman Zadeh*	3.00

HEALTH

—DR. LINDNER'S SPECIAL WEIGHT CONTROL METHOD	1.50
—HELP YOURSELF TO BETTER SIGHT *Margaret Darst Corbett*	3.00
—HOW TO IMPROVE YOUR VISION *Dr. Robert A. Kraskin*	2.00
—HOW YOU CAN STOP SMOKING PERMANENTLY *Ernest Caldwell*	2.00
—JOY OF WALKING *Jack Scagnetti*	3.00
—MIND OVER PLATTER *Peter G. Lindner, M.D.*	3.00
—NATURE'S WAY TO NUTRITION & VIBRANT HEALTH *Robert J. Scrutton*	3.00
—NEW CARBOHYDRATE DIET COUNTER *Patti Lopez-Pereira*	1.50
—PSYCHEDELIC ECSTASY *William Marshall & Gilbert W. Taylor*	2.00
—REFLEXOLOGY *Dr. Maybelle Segal*	2.00
—YOU CAN LEARN TO RELAX *Dr. Samuel Gutwirth*	2.00
—YOUR ALLERGY—What To Do About It *Allan Knight, M.D.*	3.00

HOBBIES

—BEACHCOMBING FOR BEGINNERS *Norman Hickin*	2.00
—BLACKSTONE'S MODERN CARD TRICKS *Harry Blackstone*	3.00
—BLACKSTONE'S SECRETS OF MAGIC *Harry Blackstone*	2.00
—BUTTERFLIES	2.50
—COIN COLLECTING FOR BEGINNERS *Burton Hobson & Fred Reinfeld*	2.00
—ENTERTAINING WITH ESP *Tony 'Doc' Shiels*	2.00
—400 FASCINATING MAGIC TRICKS YOU CAN DO *Howard Thurston*	3.00
—GOULD'S GOLD & SILVER GUIDE TO COINS *Maurice Gould*	2.00
—HOW I TURN JUNK INTO FUN AND PROFIT *Sari*	3.00
—HOW TO PLAY THE HARMONICA FOR FUN AND PROFIT *Hal Leighton*	3.00
—HOW TO WRITE A HIT SONG & SELL IT *Tommy Boyce*	7.00
—JUGGLING MADE EASY *Rudolf Dittrich*	2.00
—MAGIC MADE EASY *Byron Wels*	2.00
—STAMP COLLECTING FOR BEGINNERS *Burton Hobson*	2.00
—STAMP COLLECTING FOR FUN & PROFIT *Frank Cetin*	2.00

HORSE PLAYERS' WINNING GUIDES

—BETTING HORSES TO WIN *Les Conklin*	3.00
—ELIMINATE THE LOSERS *Bob McKnight*	3.00
—HOW TO PICK WINNING HORSES *Bob McKnight*	3.00
—HOW TO WIN AT THE RACES *Sam (The Genius) Lewin*	3.00
—HOW YOU CAN BEAT THE RACES *Jack Kavanagh*	3.00

___SEX WITHOUT GUILT *Albert Ellis, Ph.D.*	3.00
___SEXUALLY ADEQUATE MALE *Frank S. Caprio, M.D.*	3.00

METAPHYSICS & OCCULT

___BOOK OF TALISMANS, AMULETS & ZODIACAL GEMS *William Pavitt*	4.00
___CONCENTRATION—A Guide to Mental Mastery *Mouni Sadhu*	3.00
___CRITIQUES OF GOD *Edited by Peter Angeles*	7.00
___DREAMS & OMENS REVEALED *Fred Gettings*	3.00
___EXTRASENSORY PERCEPTION *Simeon Edmunds*	2.00
___EXTRA-TERRESTRIAL INTELLIGENCE—The First Encounter	6.00
___FORTUNE TELLING WITH CARDS *P. Foli*	2.00
___HANDWRITING ANALYSIS MADE EASY *John Marley*	3.00
___HANDWRITING TELLS *Nadya Olyanova*	5.00
___HOW TO UNDERSTAND YOUR DREAMS *Geoffrey A. Dudley*	2.00
___ILLUSTRATED YOGA *William Zorn*	3.00
___IN DAYS OF GREAT PEACE *Mouni Sadhu*	3.00
___KING SOLOMON'S TEMPLE IN THE MASONIC TRADITION *Alex Horne*	5.00
___LSD—THE AGE OF MIND *Bernard Roseman*	2.00
___MAGICIAN—His training and work *W. E. Butler*	2.00
___MEDITATION *Mouni Sadhu*	4.00
___MODERN NUMEROLOGY *Morris C. Goodman*	3.00
___NUMEROLOGY—ITS FACTS AND SECRETS *Ariel Yvon Taylor*	3.00
___PALMISTRY MADE EASY *Fred Gettings*	3.00
___PALMISTRY MADE PRACTICAL *Elizabeth Daniels Squire*	3.00
___PALMISTRY SECRETS REVEALED *Henry Frith*	2.00
___PRACTICAL YOGA *Ernest Wood*	3.00
___PROPHECY IN OUR TIME *Martin Ebon*	2.50
___PSYCHOLOGY OF HANDWRITING *Nadya Olyanova*	3.00
___SUPERSTITION—Are you superstitious? *Eric Maple*	2.00
___TAROT *Mouni Sadhu*	5.00
___TAROT OF THE BOHEMIANS *Papus*	5.00
___TEST YOUR ESP *Martin Ebon*	2.00
___WAYS TO SELF-REALIZATION *Mouni Sadhu*	3.00
___WHAT YOUR HANDWRITING REVEALS *Albert E. Hughes*	2.00
___WITCHCRAFT, MAGIC & OCCULTISM—A Fascinating History *W. B. Crow*	5.00
___WITCHCRAFT—THE SIXTH SENSE *Justine Glass*	3.00
___WORLD OF PSYCHIC RESEARCH *Hereward Carrington*	2.00
___YOU CAN ANALYZE HANDWRITING *Robert Holder*	2.00

SELF-HELP & INSPIRATIONAL

___CYBERNETICS WITHIN US *Y. Saparina*	3.00
___DAILY POWER FOR JOYFUL LIVING *Dr. Donald Curtis*	3.00
___DOCTOR PSYCHO-CYBERNETICS *Maxwell Maltz, M.D.*	3.00
___DYNAMIC THINKING *Melvin Powers*	2.00
___EXUBERANCE—Your Guide to Happiness & Fulfillment *Dr. Paul Kurtz*	3.00
___GREATEST POWER IN THE UNIVERSE *U. S. Andersen*	4.00
___GROW RICH WHILE YOU SLEEP *Ben Sweetland*	3.00
___GROWTH THROUGH REASON *Albert Ellis, Ph.D.*	4.00
___GUIDE TO DEVELOPING YOUR POTENTIAL *Herbert A. Otto, Ph.D.*	3.00
___GUIDE TO LIVING IN BALANCE *Frank S. Caprio, M.D.*	2.00
___HELPING YOURSELF WITH APPLIED PSYCHOLOGY *R. Henderson*	2.00
___HELPING YOURSELF WITH PSYCHIATRY *Frank S. Caprio, M.D.*	2.00
___HOW TO ATTRACT GOOD LUCK *A. H. Z. Carr*	3.00
___HOW TO CONTROL YOUR DESTINY *Norvell*	3.00
___HOW TO DEVELOP A WINNING PERSONALITY *Martin Panzer*	3.00
___HOW TO DEVELOP AN EXCEPTIONAL MEMORY *Young & Gibson*	4.00
___HOW TO OVERCOME YOUR FEARS *M. P. Leahy, M.D.*	3.00
___HOW YOU CAN HAVE CONFIDENCE AND POWER *Les Giblin*	3.00
___HUMAN PROBLEMS & HOW TO SOLVE THEM *Dr. Donald Curtis*	3.00
___I CAN *Ben Sweetland*	4.00
___I WILL *Ben Sweetland*	3.00
___LEFT-HANDED PEOPLE *Michael Barsley*	3.00